# Quilt Restoration

## A Practical Guide

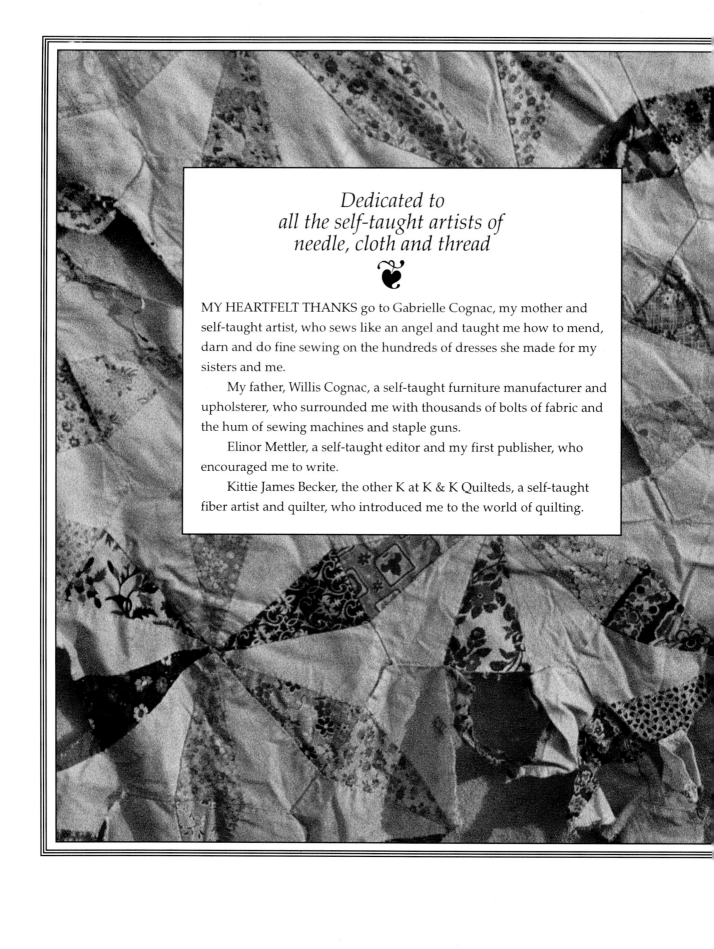

*Dedicated to
all the self-taught artists of
needle, cloth and thread*

❦

MY HEARTFELT THANKS go to Gabrielle Cognac, my mother and self-taught artist, who sews like an angel and taught me how to mend, darn and do fine sewing on the hundreds of dresses she made for my sisters and me.

My father, Willis Cognac, a self-taught furniture manufacturer and upholsterer, who surrounded me with thousands of bolts of fabric and the hum of sewing machines and staple guns.

Elinor Mettler, a self-taught editor and my first publisher, who encouraged me to write.

Kittie James Becker, the other K at K & K Quilteds, a self-taught fiber artist and quilter, who introduced me to the world of quilting.

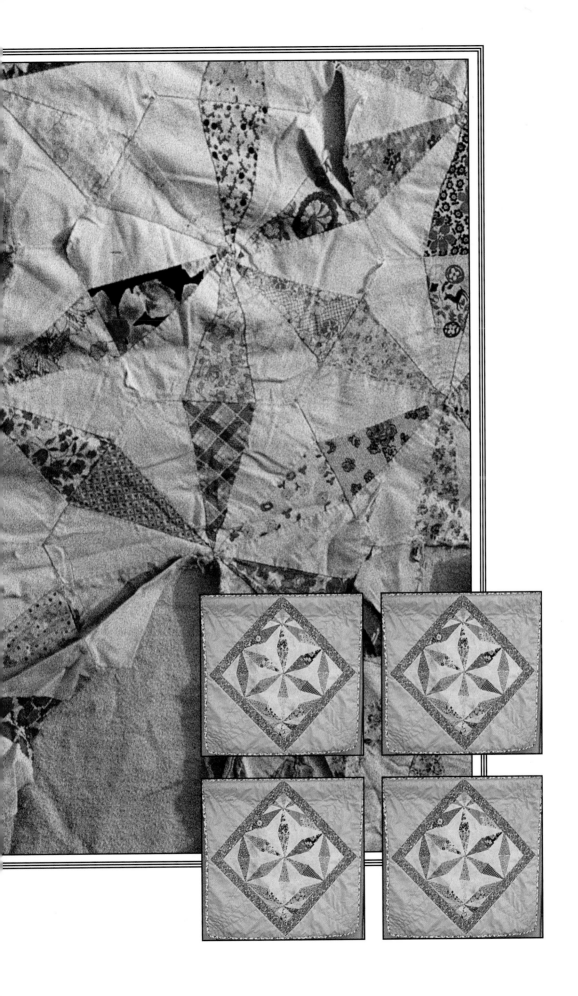

# Quilt Restoration
## A Practical Guide

CAMILLE DALPHOND COGNAC

EPM

McLean, Virginia

Library of Congress Cataloging-in-Publication Data
Cognac, Camille Dalphond.
    Quilt restoration : a practical guide / Camille Dalphond Cognac.
      p.  cm.
    Includes bibliographical references.
    ISBN 0-939009-83-8
      1. Quilts——Conservation and restoration.  2. Quilts——Repairing.  I. Title.
TT835.C634  1994
746.46'0488——dc20                                 94-35126
                                                      CIP

EPM Publications, Inc., 1003 Turkey Run Road
 McLean, VA 22101
Printed in the United States of America

First Printing, September 1994

Cover and book design by Tom Huestis
Author photo by David R. Shetsky

# Contents

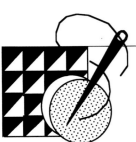

# Restoration and Conservation: The Difference

QUILT RESTORATION has always existed. Practicality and common sense have always motivated people to fix, repair or mend the objects used in their daily lives. Ever since cloth was first woven, all people have devised ways of extending the life of sails, bags, garments, quilts and home furnishings. Every object made with cloth becomes worn in time, and simple methods of mending, darning and patching have been universally applied to maintain an object's usability.

The same patient repetition of simple stitches seen on a sail remnant used to wrap an Egyptian mummy are used to repair an 1880s quilt or a Victorian wedding dress. Whether the fabric used is hand-blocked vintage fabric or a quality reproduction, the methods used are the same. Whether a quilt is restored in a studio setting or on the dining room table, the methods are still the same.

Twenty five years of sewing–dressmaking, remodeling, designing–prepared me for quilt restoration. When first asked to fix a quilt, I brought a common sense approach to repairing the damage. Unburdened by a prescribed list of dos and don'ts, I used many of the same methods over and over because they worked. Using rules of balance and symmetry, I made repairs in such a way as to create balance in each quilt, just as one would create balance in a dress or blazer.

Twelve years ago, I did not separate quilts from the larger context of sewing with needle, cloth and thread. Now, having repaired thousands of quilts and read hundreds of books on the historical development of quilting throughout the world and having broadened my acquaintance with printed textiles, I bring more knowledge to quilt restoration. Although I have more knowledge on which to base decisions than previously, I still apply the same methods I used 12 years ago because these methods, as I said above, are the universal solutions for all fabric.

Ninety percent of all quilt restoration requires simple sewing skills that revolve around mending, darning and patching. These old-fashioned words are the universal base of all textile repair across the centuries. When a fabric is weakened through use or dye tendering, something needs to be done to stabilize or

*Reverse Applique Oak Leaf in Garden Maze, c. 1850. Rainbow print was used to repair this quilt. The minute stitches and threads indicate an early repair, perhaps even by the original quiltmaker.*

replace it so that the damage does not advance. Hence the old adage: A stitch in time saves nine.

Hundreds of the antique quilts I have seen have been mended, darned and patched. They were simply being maintained by the owner so that they could still be used or preserved. Interestingly, the majority of the vintage clothing and household linens I have seen have also been mended, darned and patched in the same manner. Quilts were always made within the larger context of household linens and were always repaired in a similar fashion.

In 1640 England, John Taylor's poem, "The Praise of the Needle," was already in its twelfth edition because of its popularity among English needlewomen. His praise is still apropos today:

*A Needle (though it be but*
*small and slender)*
*Yet it is both a maker and a mender:*
*A graue (sic) Reformer of old*
*Rents decayd,*
*Stops holes and seames,*
*and desperate cuts displayed.* [1]

Great grandma never asked permission to cut down Johnny's tattered quilt to fit little Betsy's cradle. She simply cut away the damaged sections and rebound the salvaged section into a child or doll quilt. Great grandma may also have preserved a wedding applique quilt which was never used except for special occasions. Across the centuries, quilts have been both preserved and used. Quality quilts from the 1840s often surface in pristine condition because they were cherished; utilitarian quilts from 1930, on the other hand, can be threadbare, stained and tattered.

Quilts were darned, patched and rebacked over and over again until their overall condition relegated them to mattress or vegetable covers. They were expected to wear out because they were an ordinary part of daily life. Their ordinariness is precisely what made them so versatile.

---

"Get some old quilts and go wrap them pipes good," my mother would say. "It's going to get down cold tonight." In many cases these "Old quilts were permanently wrapped around the pipes and remained there for many years as superior insulation.

The uses for old quilts are almost unending. Then great grandmother's quilt went through its second or third incarnation and became just too tattered and torn for any other purpose, it could always be used as the dog's bed. . . .Old quilts seem never to die a sudden death. An old pair of shoes might be tossed in the trash can, but I don't remember seeing an old quilt disposed of in such manner. They just keep being relegated to a lower use, until they are no more. [2]

---

Utilitarian quilts tend to be badly repaired with make-do fabric and oversized patches. As practical items they were patched quickly to be used as soon as possible. Show quilts are beautifully restored using meticulous reweaving and almost perfect fabric matches.

Quilt restoration techniques over the last 150 years reflect the quilt owner's perception of the quilt. Quilts seen as necessary household objects were consistently repaired with dispatch. The function of a utilitarian quilt is more important than its visual appearance. The appearance of an heirloom quilt is more important than its function. Just as a wedding gown would be meticulously reworked for a later bride, so would a masterpiece quilt be painstakingly restored to its original beauty. Work pants, on the other hand, would be quickly patched like an everyday quilt.

Grouping all quilts together as equally precious is a current romanticized view of quilts which denies reality. Two kinds of quilts have always co-existed: functional and decorative—or plain and fancy. A tattered and stained Sears housedress is not a Dior gown, and to treat them as if they were of equal quality defies common sense.

Across the country, closets, drawers and under-bed storage boxes hide ragged and torn family quilts. Ashamed to throw them out and ashamed to display them, quilt owners don't know what to do. Common sense says they are not worth saving, but family sentiment will not allow throwing them out.

Country auctions, tag sales and flea markets abound with ragamuffin quilts that beckon us to do something to rescue them from the landfill. Too fragmented to be used as moving pads and too damaged to be patched, these problem quilts nevertheless speak to our hearts. Any handmade object in our highly mechanized society touches our human need to be connected to other human beings. Handmade objects, knitted, woven, sewn or quilted, nourish our tactile and emotional needs to be swathed in love and comfort. From the cradle to the grave, we are wrapped in textiles. Is it any wonder that these quilts have such a deep emotional hold on us?

Problem quilts whether family owned or bought at auction need loving care, some guidance and much patience to be transformed into beauties. Many quilt restoration solutions offered in this guide pertain to these kinds of problem quilts, waiting like ugly ducklings to be transformed into swans.

# Quilt Restoration

In England, a clear distinction is made between conservation and restoration of textiles. According to Karen Finch and Greta Putnam, England's leading experts at the Textile Conservation Centre: "Conservation requires that everything that is original on an object be retained, and nothing added. Restoration, on the other hand, implies a degree of repair so that the piece not only looks as nearly as it did originally but it may even be made strong enough for further use." [3]

In the United States, textile conservation guidelines are often recommended today as quilt restoration techniques. However, American conservation techniques do not meet the needs of many damaged quilts. To suggest "crepeline netting" and "acid-free storage", for example, to the owner of a quilt that is falling into pieces like flags at a car dealership is not a solution. Such a tattered quilt is not of museum quality and therefore museum guidelines need not be followed by its owners.

Owners of problem quilts for years have analyzed their own predicaments, created their own solutions (and sometimes asked to have the work done for them). Needing no degrees, they have applied common sense to a very real problem and have been responsible for many creative solutions. The quilt restoration techniques described in the following chapters address the grand canyon which exists today between rigid conservation techniques and the indiscriminate cutting of damaged quilts into bunnies with moving eyes.

Restoration has always existed in the art and antique world. The word restore comes from the Latin root, restaurare, meaning to renew and to rebuild. Stone, wood, stained glass and paintings have been restored professionally for centuries. If one can restore the Sistine chapel with paint and brushes, one can restore quilts with cloth and thread. As Kaethe Kliot of the Lacis Studio states so clearly, "You cannot sew onto nothing." [4]

Until the early 1970s, very few people cared what was done with quilts. Used as blankets for moving and sold for $5 a piece, quilts were largely unappreciated and dismissed as women's work. Likewise, quilt restoration remained a hidden art within the home and was seen as mending, darning and patching. Mend, a four-letter word, seemingly reduces hours of meticulous restoration to kitchen-corner mending-basket work and all too easily denigrates the skillful restoration that has been practiced in homes for centuries.

Quilt restoration evolved from the same context as clothing restoration, remodeling and alteration. For centuries, damaged clothing was re-fashioned as a way of saving what good material remained and early general sewing books included sections on remodeling. Clothing alteration requires shortening or lengthening the garment to suit the wearer; clothing repair and remodeling often requires stealing fabric from the garment in order to give it back to the garment. Ordinary dressmaking accepts interfacings and fusing agents. All such home-sewing techniques and solutions need to be re-examined for adaptability to quilt restoration.

Jonathan Holstein states: "Quiltmaking was a salvage art." Likewise, quilt restoration is a salvage art, which requires decision making about what to keep and what to eliminate. Holstein correctly assesses quiltmaking as a compromise with necessity which assembled something utilitarian from available materials. [5] Many quilters were artists who by necessity combined function with beauty. Quilt owners today face the same challenge when a quilt may

be seen vertically as an art piece or horizontally as a bed quilt. Any damage challenges our creativity in the same way that fabric scraps challenged the earlier quiltmakers.

Quilts as art require an artist's eye and even the most damaged fragment of a quilt can be presented in such a way as to enhance its inherent beauty or primitive charm. While rereading old quilt magazines, I noticed a common sense approach to severely damaged quilts. Helen King happily shared her salvaging of a damaged Rose of Sharon into a smaller quilt, pillow and vest, while Ann Wittells enthusiastically listed dozens of salvage possibilities for severely damaged quilts. Wittell's suggestions range from large to small and are exactly what quilt owners request today.

*The Fine Art of Quilting showcases clothing, pillows and small bags in a 1920 photo found in a shoe box. Quilted items were praised across the centuries for their decorative flair as well as warmth. Author's collection.*

In *The Romance of the Patchwork Quilt in America*, Carrie Hall and Rose G. Kretsinger took great delight in describing "thrifty housewives" who converted heavily quilted petticoats (jupon) from the 1700s "into coverlets by sewing two lengths together." The French quilt jupon later became "little quilted boudoir pillows, made from the scraps of material left after covering a chair or couch. These gay old petticoats were not only used to cover furniture, but because of their lovely, picturesque and colorful patterns, were put to many other uses: boudoir jackets, portieres and drapes of different kinds ."[6]

American pioneer quiltmakers used damaged quilts as battings for other quilts, insulation against the cold and vegetable covers. The 1880s *Housekeeping Manual* recommends cutting up old quilts for use as pads under stair rugs. Although extreme, this last example underscores a thrifty householder's wish to make good use of a quilt which had lost its original purpose. Fortunately, there are many better solutions for such problem quilts today.

# Quilt Restoration Guidelines

The practical options and creative problem solving techniques which are explored in the following chapters should be read like recipes in a cookbook. The reader is free to choose which suggestions are best suited for any particular quilt. Ten quilts may evoke ten different solutions because quilts, like children, are individual unto themselves.

" The key to restoration is research. Familiarizing yourself with a project is the key to doing a good job. You look ahead, then proceed with caution."

R. Agass Baumgartner
Baumgartner Fine Art Restoration

Quilt owners wish to be assured the quilt information given is valid and for this reason, I will refer to the definitive text on identifying and dating antique quilts, *Clues in the Calico* by Barbara Brackman. Because Brackman's information about fabric, dyes, styles and techniques is historically correct, it is the most valid text on the history of quiltmaking in the United States. Over 75% of all historical information about quilts is highly romanticized and incorrect. Brackman attributes this to "the quantity of inaccurate, out-of-date and out-of-print literature still in libraries." Quilt historians were often misled by misinformation from an earlier generation of writers who romanticized and inadvertently falsified the history of quiltmaking.[7] Brackman's scientific approach and carefully researched information rests on fact rather than fiction and I will refer to her *Clues in the Calico* for supplemental historical reading for readers who want to learn more.

With silhouettes of George and Martha Washington flanking the title, a Log Cabin quilt-pillow is assumed to stem from Colonial days when, in fact, it did not appear until the 1860s. Thus has much quilt history been romanticized.

# How perception of a quilt c

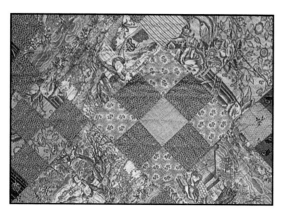

## PERCEPTION

What may appear to you as simple design with odd color combinations could deceive you into thinking this is an ordinary scrap quilt with less than great colors.

## FACT

**Toile de Jouy Quilt.**
Rare early 1800s quilt with inked inscription describing great grandmother's bed curtain toile, which was engraved in France.
(78, 79, 88)*

## PERCEPTION

Quilt's mint condition and fresh look make it look new. Thought of as grandma's quilt rather than earlier. Nothing so clean could be nearly 150 years old!

## FACT

**Rose of Sharon**
Floral Applique with swag border and fine quilting. Color and design suggest that this quilt was a wedding quilt c. 1850.
(142-3, 155-7, 173)*

## PERCEPTION

Wool, some moth eaten, and simple design could easily be judged as working man's quilt from early 1900 made from suiting fabrics. Weight suggests a crude quilt.

## FACT

**Linsey Woolsey.**
Rare late 1700s quilt which weighs 10 pounds, has wool batting and calimanco glazed wool. Stab stitch and cut out for bed with piping.
(48, 134-5)*

*All page references are to *Clues in the Calico* by Barbara Brackman

## PERCEPTION

Cross hatch handquilting is so precise that it looks like a mattress pad when folded. Design could be applied to mattress cover. Dye rot, dye migration and soil would not make this quilt appreciated in most homes.

## FACT

**Tree of Life**.
Rare, cut-out chintz applique, also called Broderie Perse from late 1700s. Hand-stamped fabric is appliqued to imitate palampores from India.
(19, 35, 81-9, 101-3, 104, 124, 126-7, 135-6)*

# ffer from the facts about it

### PERCEPTION
Pastel colors suggest a 1920–30 quilt when Lone Star quilt kits were all the rage. Silk separates it from the norm, but velvet flowers might easily place the quilt in the 1880s when Lone Stars were made in silk and velvet.

### FACT
**Medallion Lone Star.**
Rare Pre-Civil War quilt of imported silk with circular medallion of velvet and silk flowers and leaves which resemble English stumpwork from 17th and 18th century.
(41-3, 141, 115, 171)*

### PERCEPTION
A heavy, irregular, mis-matched mess of a thing. Why would anyone spend time making this ripple horror? Like a wacky rug using too many colors, it would be an eye sore in most homes.

### FACT
**Target Quilt, c. 1930.**
Prairie Points are built up in concentric circles in undulating three dimensional ripples. This collector's quilt speaks of freedom, individuality and decades of fabric. Its uniqueness makes it a prized collector or museum quilt.

### PERCEPTION
Both quilts come from the same time because they use the same design. Design, however, does not mandate the historical setting so much as fabric and finishing methods do.

### FACT
**Honeycomb, 1850 and Grandmother's Flower Garden,1930.**
Both use the hexagonal shape which the Godey's book called honeycomb in 1835 and which resurfaced in silk during the 1880s and again in pastels in the 1930s.
(128, 169)*

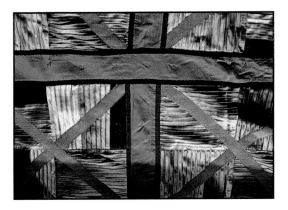

### PERCEPTION
Avocado Green! A horror of the avacado rage in the '60s. Did someone really make this? Why is this stuff pleated and why did she use cheap blanket binding and sew over grosgrain ribbon? Ugh! This amalgam of fabrics would clash in serene settings.

### FACT
**Pleated Rainbow Quilt.**
Ribbons, blanket bindings and pleated silk samples are joined with textural splendor. Did the maker have access to dressmaking samples from a friend or work in a notions factory? Like all collector quilts, this 1910 quilt sparkles with the quiltmaker's individuality.

I have deliberately avoided including historical information about quilts and technical information about quiltmaking. Hundreds of books are available on both subjects, and many quilt owners are neither historians, nor quiltmakers. The techniques described in the following chapters require simple sewing skills, common sense and patience.

The first questions to be asked before any decision is made about restoring a damaged quilt are:

1. What is the quilt's historical importance?
2. When was it made?
3. Should anything be done with it?
4. What is its as-is value?

No one quilt dealer, book, quilt shop owner or antique expert can answer all these questions. However, if many dealers, antique experts, quilt owners and books repeatedly give similar information, then the quilt owner can slowly gain a body of knowledge about the quilt.

Fifteen years ago my own lack of knowledge about the chronological development of patterns, fabrics and methods was such that I would not have known the value or rarity of any quilt; my ignorance affected my perception of a quilt. The simplicity of earlier designs and the variety in aging of fabrics also affected my perceptions. The more I learned, the easier it became to avoid making decisions about restoration that would be regretted later. In the box shown on pages 14 and 15 you see some examples of what I mean.

# Different Approaches to Restoration

As has been noted, people own, admire and cherish quilts for many reasons, and each quilt owner will make decisions about restorations based on personal feelings about his/her quilts. Before making final decisions, you should ask yourself what your own approach is toward quilts. The categories listed below may help you decide which restoration route you want to take.

## Utilitarian Quilts

Some people own and admire quilts for their use on beds. They snuggle up under them for warmth; they admire their hand crafted beauty and appreciate the homey feeling imparted. These quilt lovers need practical and sturdy quilts for their daily use which, of course, is the quilt's original purpose.

## Art Quilts

Some people own and admire quilts as art. They hang them on walls, in foyers, dens and dining areas. They drape them on banisters and dowels. They stare at these handcrafted beauties and wonder if the quiltmaker ever perceived the full power and impact the quilt held. They fondle; they touch; they breathe in the quilt's beauty and they are nourished daily by their hanging quilts.

## Family Quilts

Family quilts are often treasured and protected. On special occasions, these family heirlooms are taken out of the blanket chests, drawers and closets to be displayed and shared. Preserving one's family heritage has strong significance within such homes and guarantees that cherished quilts will be enjoyed by future generations.

### Collector Quilts

Some people cherish quilts in museum and private collections. Like sphinx guarding their royal charges, they preserve and protect their quilts for thousands to enjoy, admire and study. Just as visitors go to see royal jewels or Medici tapestries in museums around the world, so also do visitors go to admire and appreciate quilts. Thousands of them go to learn about textile history preserved within collections.

### Dealer Quilts

Some people own, buy and sell quilts. Enamored of textiles, they rescue quilts from attics, basements and barns. They search for quilts in flea markets, auctions and tag sales. They often save quilts from landfills, rodents and natural disintegration. Like archeologists they find artifacts of our past that have remained hidden for decades or even centuries and given them new life.

### Challenge Quilts

A few people are magnetically attracted to problem quilts which no one else seems to want. Often these are multi-generational quilts worked on by two or three quiltmakers who kept adding their flair. Some may have been made by poor seamstresses with no artistic sense or skill. Loved because they are wacky or imbalanced, the problem quilts tug at the heart like disheveled children in mismatched clothes.

A cherished family quilt will often be painstakingly restored, even if such a project requires 300 hours. Such a quilt can require vintage fabric and exact replication of the family heirloom, unlike a utilitarian quilt that may easily accept reproduction fabric.

Art quilts may need to be prepared for framing so that the frayed fabrics remain in place. The challenge quilt may need to be minimized and bordered in order to contain its erratic piecing. The dealer quilt could have mouse-chewed holes or fabric losses that have to be repaired. And a collector quilt will be prepared for safekeeping in a temperature controlled setting for continued study.

Quilt owners may find the chart on page 18 helpful in considering possibilities for their quilts. Damage varies from quilt to quilt. Important historical quilts may have damage, but their historical significance makes the as-is damage acceptable for the owner or collector, whereas utilitarian quilts with severe damage may require more drastic techniques.

Double vision is required of all quilt lovers, collectors and quilters who read this book. The quilt restoration techniques given here are for the quilt lover who wishes to own and appreciate quilts in day-to-day living and who is enough of a dreamer and artist to see what a quilt could be. The methods described are varied and optional because quilts, like people, are unique. Quilt restoration must be seen as a labor of love in which the restorer becomes a co-creator with the original quiltmaker.

Like Janus, the Roman deity who symbolizes wholeness, the quilt restorer must look to the past as well as to the future. Janus, with his double vision, denoted both awareness of history and foreknowledge. Seeing in both directions Janus brought a depth of understanding to events. Some quilts are to be

## Aid to Deciding Whether to Restore, Conserve or Salvage

**H**=Horizontal  **V**=Vertical  **C**=Conservation  **R**=Restoration  **S**=Salvage

| Quilt Types | Quilt Purpose | Damage 5-25% | Damage 25-50% | Damage over 50% |
|---|---|---|---|---|
| Utilitarian | daily use, H | R | R/S | S |
| Art | display, V | R/S | R/S | S |
| Family | display, H/V preserve | C/R | C/R | R/S |
| Collector | preserve display, H/V | R/C | C | C |
| Dealer | buy/ sell for use /display | C/R/S | C/R/S | C/R/S* |
| Challenge | display use, H/V | C/R/S | C/R/S | C/R/S* |

\* Unusual historical pieces—whether badly made or purchased for resale—ask to be conserved for their historical significance. Research and study by the quilt owner will indicate the rarity. Many dealers show great sensitivity to these unusual quilts.

preserved as historical documents and require museum conservation techniques; others that are to be enjoyed in daily life require quilt restoration techniques. May Janus' double-vision approach grant us the privilege of knowing the difference.

## Quilt Restoration Primer

At this time, much of the information available for textile preservation pertains to museum settings only and aims to preserve and document the textile or quilt for further study, not for use in homes. In her article, "Resurrecting a Family Treasure, "Linda Hearn tells how she dealt with her dilemma." As a first step, I consulted with experts," she writes. "I learned that they perform washing, mounting and fumigation procedures along with collection surveys and laboratory examinations. However, their primary function is preservation of textiles rather than repair and restoration. So I was on my own to determine the extent of repairs required." [8]

# Desecration of a Peony Quilt

In the first quarter of the 20th century, many old unfinished quilt tops and squares were put together quickly and cheaply. In short, they were finished for functional use. Such multi-generational quilts often have a clashing quality to them and are examples of make-do quilt restoration at its worst. Whoever finished them omitted steps 2 and 4 of the methodology on p. 20. The original quilt top made of pieced red fabric and applique leaves indicate a pre-Civil War vintage. The Shelburne Museum has a dated peony quilt from 1841, and the tiny applique stitches and 1850s red print fabric indicate an early completion.

During the 1930s this quilt top was crudely quilted with utilitarian batting and the quiltmaker thought so little of the large quilt top, she folded over the top of the quilt twice in order to use the actual quilt as a chin and hand protector.

The quilt was no doubt laundered repeatedly and used as an everyday quilt because it was damaged severely by abrasion and washing. During the 1960s a later enthusiast, with little skill, decided to cover over the damage by basting large pieces of red and white star polycotton print over the existing red damage. Not all the red peonies were covered, but, certainly enough to add sparkle to the last desecration of this 1850s quilt top, which is now almost comical because it has been repeatedly abused by quilt owners.

Examples like these of wholesale desecration of old quilts create a valid fear among contemporary quilt historians. However, we no longer live in the same geographic and social isolation which once prohibited the sharing of resources and knowledge. Research sources are readily available to all quilt restorers who choose to know about a quilt and its historical significance.

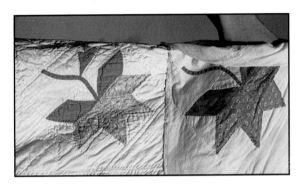

*Peony Quilt reflects 100 year history from 1860-1960. Several owners made poor finishing choices. In 1930s the top was hand quilted in a utilitarian manner and two rows were turned under to form a double-sided chin protector.*

*Later, in 1960, polycotton red and white star fabric was crudely applied to cover the damage from harsh use and repeated launderings.*

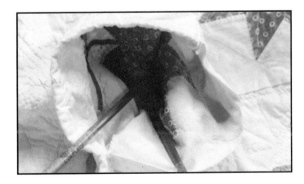

*Chopstick points to appliqued lily block that had been covered when two top rows were folded under. No doubt the original quiltmaker of the meticulously pieced lily did not intend for her handwork to be hidden.*

With further research, she "found little published on the topic," except conservation guidelines which require that "repairs should be reversible." Because the damaged quilt needed reworking in order to be usable, Hearn formulated "a personal theory about the restoration of quilts." Her theory is valid for all restorers: "My view is that a quilt is meant to be enjoyed by someone who loves it." Following her own guideline, she successfully repaired the damaged quilt. She closes her article by pointing out "the need for more information on quilt restoration." It should be pointed out that quilt restoration techniques and guidelines already do exist; however, they have not been stated as clearly as they could be. While researching through hundreds of quilt books and magazines for this book, I came upon two articles that haunted me: "The Garbage Can Quilt and Other Lovelies" by Aloyse Yorko [9] and "Sister Quilts from Sicily: A Pair of Renaissance Bedcovers" by Susan Young. [10] Although both articles appeared at first to be disconnected from each other, I felt compelled to read them over and over again as if I were missing the point of my obsession. What does a garbage can quilt have to do with a 14th-century quilt related to the show-piece quilt in the Victoria and Albert Museum? These articles wouldn't leave me alone until I deciphered their secret connection.

Eureka! I suddenly realized that these two authors had repeated the same methods followed by Hearn. Both Yorko and Young experienced first hand the very same process:

## Methodology

1. Chance discovery
2. Research about quilt
3. Wish to rescue
4. Historical research
5. Decision
6. Sharing with others

Yorko states: "I hold strongly to the belief that if a person dreams long enough about something, it just might happen." Both Yorko's and Young's dreams came true.

One morning, Yorko found a gift quilt in a garbage can and decided this castoff was "a thing of beauty that deserved to be rescued and loved." Young, a New Zealand quilter, felt the same imperative to research and rescue a 14th-century Sicilian quilt which she chanced upon years ago in Florence, Italy. Yorko's quilt rose from its garbage can obscurity to be shared with quilters all over the world, and Young's "undervalued and neglected" quilt was publicly acknowledged as the sister quilt to the Victoria and Albert Museum showpiece, known as the earliest existing quilt.

The common thread binding these two quilt lovers does not end, but continues throughout both articles. Both women used sleuth-like skills to dig, analyze and hypothesize about the quilts. Both persisted in their need to resolve and clarify; they both reflected on the maker and the method of the making. In short, the quilts just wouldn't leave them alone. Both women wanted the quilts to fall into the right hands so that they would be properly cared for in the future.

Linda Hearn followed the exact same procedure when she worked on her family-owned damaged quilt. Finding no guidelines,

Hearn did what all quilt lovers and quilt restorers have been doing for centuries. This almost scientific procedure is a classic formula for all effective problem solving in quilt restoration.

Young had never planned on researching Renaissance manuscripts; however, she did so in order to find out more information. Most quilt restorers don't plan to research the effect of metal used on fabric in the 1800s, nor do they plan to search out arcane books on mending and darning; but problems ask to be solved. Yorko never planned on finding the quilt in the garbage can, but she did. People don't expect to inherit damaged quilts, but they do.

# How to Start a Restoration

It isn't necessary for a quilt restorer to write an article, but steps 1—5 of the methodology are crucial. In addition to following these basic steps, you will need certain basic attributes:

## What It Takes

Motivation
Patience
Common sense
Ability to imitate
Simple sewing skills

Motivation is more important for quilt restoration than any previous training. Once motivated, one achieves the necessary skills through practice and desire to learn.

Quilt restoration is so labor intensive that the concept of competion hardly enters in. My hands, highly trained, can only move so

fast and still do fine work. Because there are thousands of damaged quilts in need of 50 to 200 hours of labor each, one can easily realize the enormity of the challenge for quilt restorers.

## Books to the Rescue

Here are basic titles that will help you:

*The Mender's Manual*, Foote
*The Care & Preservation of Textiles*,
    Finch and Putnam
*Quilter's Complete Guide*,
    Fons and Porter
*Clues in the Calico*, Brackman

## Fabrics and Supplies

If I were an old quilt or quilt top, I would want to be discovered at this time. Never before have there been so many sources available for vintage fabrics and supplies. Never have there been such beautiful reproduction fabrics in 100% cotton, and never has there been such sensitivity and reverence for quilts. There are so many resources that I devote all of Chapter X and the Bibliography to help you find them.

Margo Krager of Patchworks in Manhattan, Montana is now able to offer shirting fabric, for example, that is reproduced in the old traditional way as well as real "flour sacking." Jeannie Spears has shared her discovery of late 1800s fabrics being sold today in South Africa that are produced for that market far away in England. This English fabric is exactly the same as the 1800s fabrics and made on the same old rollers.[11] Hilary Ostlere writes of the Whitchurch Silk Mill nestled in the English countryside which is producing silk exactly as it did 160 years ago. [12] Hand-stamped William Morris fabric is also being made just as it was in the late 1800s. [13]

Thanks to generous networking among quilters, these time-capsuled discoveries are available all over the world to anyone who writes a letter or picks up the phone. The Kirk Collection in Omaha, Nebraska, for example, carries 10,000 yards of vintage fabric at any given time; the Northhampton Textile Company, newly opened in Massachusetts, specializes in vintage fabrics and beads; LACIS in Berkeley, California carries antique laces, hundreds of specialized textile books and over a thousand sewing specialty items. I may not be able to go to Berkeley, Omaha or Montana from my upstate New York town, but, for the cost of a four-hour car trip, I can call, order and receive the needed item the next day. As the need for these supplies grows, so will the network and even more choices will become available. I project that by the time this book is read there will be a dozen or more resources available to quilt restorers.

While writing the book I have been privileged to speak with quilt restorers across the country. Knowledgeable and skillful, these dedicated women bring to quilt restoration both the eyes of artists who can see beyond the damage as well as the skill which comes from years of self-training and hands-on practice. Without a network to guide them, they have amassed a vast repertoire of restoration skills. Fine quilt restoration comes from the heart which feels an affinity with the quilt and the original quiltmaker. To restore an antique quilt is to belong to a long tradition of needlework which transcends any particular place or time.

Most restoration projects are true labors of love in which the restorer becomes a co-creator with the original quiltmaker. Susan McLennan Anderson has described her experience beautifully: "I have one 19th century quilt in my collection that is approximately 10 feet long by 10-½ feet wide. The piecework is the Star of Bethlehem. . . .The outstanding feature of this quilt is its formidable background, entirely and elaborately trapunto-stitched with 10 to 12 stitches per inch. This quilt is done entirely by one person and it was obviously her masterpiece. For my part it took over a year's spare time to restore. . . .I purchased this quilt for only $250 due to the stains, the grime and the necessary restoration. I would not part with this quilt now for ten times that amount."[14]

Major restoration projects, such as replacing 128 diamonds in a Lone Star quilt, require 128–192 hours of a quilter's time. Such commitment requires patience and pacing. Goals need to be realistic, so that the restorer doesn't become discouraged. I often tell a beginner to first accept the fact that it may take six months to two years to finish a major project.

Thousands of quilts are waiting to be discovered. Their time has come to be re-examined with new eyes. I, too, hold strongly to the belief that if a person dreams long enough about something, it just might happen. Quilts cast a hypnotic spell on our hearts. Perhaps quilts share our dreams and beckon us to see them anew.

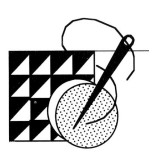

# Kinds of Major Damage

DAMAGED QUILTS EXIST. Much-loved, discarded, forgotten, they are rediscovered in attics, barns, old trunks and elsewhere. Pretending that their damage does not exist or will somehow go away not only postpones dealing with it but also accelerates the deterioration. "History doesn't stop when the quilt is finished," as Susan Hendrick Wilson says, "It just keeps happening to the quilt." [15]

What, then, does one do about damaged quilts? To bequeath heirloom status to tattered and worn utility quilts does not do justice to the many beautiful quilts, new and restored, that exist today. Although the Dior gown vs. the ragged Sears housedress controversy is rampant in the quilt world today, no one has put the final word any better than Shelly Zegart.

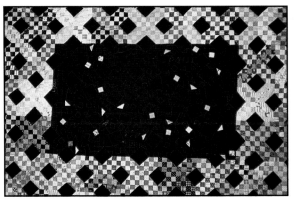

*A playful Ocean Waves which suffered central damage and was rescued by a quilter who created a central medallion wherein quilt pieces fall like confetti. Are they falling out of the border or are they finding their place within the border?*

"Unfortunately," she says, "a signed and dated ragged quilt is still a ragged quilt." [16] Bemoaning damage won't make it go away.

Damage indicates what was, but it also portends what can be. An old time quilter once told me, "My mother always said, if you ever cut your quilt by accident, applique a butterfly over the hole and make it your good luck quilt."

Looking at a severely damaged quilt, one may ask, "What can be saved from this quilt?" The question is best asked with reverence for each individual quilt. To preserve a tattered remnant of a quilt will not enhance the quilter's memory, but showcasing a good remaining section guarantees that the work can be enjoyed for generations to come, along with the memory of the quilter.

Whatever decisions are made in handling a severely damaged quilt, documentation is recommended. Taking a "before" picture and saving all the sections is important. By keeping this information along with all the sections removed from the quilt, one is preserving material that can be used for further restoration of the remaining quilt at some future time. Fifty or a hundred years from now, the saved sections may be used to repair the quilt again and thus give pleasure to yet another generation.

# Damages and Their Causes

### SINGLE-SIDE DAMAGE

Single-side, used repeatedly at head of bed was tugged, pulled and crumpled. Quilt was tucked under bed springs or received direct sunlight for years.

### CENTRAL DAMAGE

Repeated sitting on quilt caused center to become frayed right through batting into back.

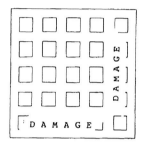

### TWO-SIDED DAMAGE

Quilt rested on bed by wall and received strong sunlight day after day. Two sides are parchment dry and have lost all resiliency. They powder or flake when toushed.

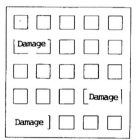

### ERRATIC DAMAGE

Some of the fabric used was overly worn when incorporated into the quilt. Dye caused cotton to self-destruct with time and laundering. Cats may have clawed at quilted fabric and left rows of tatters.

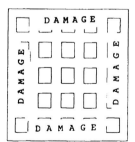

### FOUR-SIDED DAMAGE

Quilt was rotated on bed and wore from abrasion of springs and handling. Quilt was tucked under mattress repeatedly.

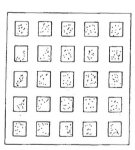

### SPECKLED DAMAGE

Two-color quilts appear to have measles because small flowers or leaves have fallen out of printed fabric with successive washings.

In deciding how to deal with damage it helps first to understand what kind it is and how it came about. In the boxed chart shown here you'll find the typical kinds of damages drawn or photographed, along with a description of their likely causes. I use the drawings again in showing how they can be repaired. I find that they help keep one's mind on solutions rather than emotions.

## Single-side, Two-sided and Four-sided Damage

**Damages 1, 2, 3** illustrated in the chart may all be repaired by rebinding the quilt using the methods described in Chapter V, Borders and Bindings. Rebinding is particularly effective when the quilt has an overall grid pattern. Instead of 25 squares, the quilt will be reduced to 20 or 16 squares.

**FLAKING DAMAGE**

Silk and silk blends from Victorian era crumple like butterfly wings.

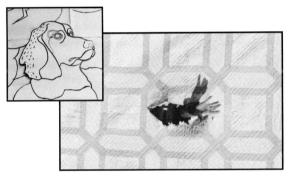

**LARGE HOLE OR HOLES**

Animal nibbled at quilt for cotton or as a way to burrow. Usually mice will leave several holes; dogs burrow into one large hole.

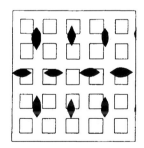

**SYMMETRICAL HOLES**

4, 8, or 16 holes appearing in symmetrical fashion are due to mice that have stolen cotton from the quilt for nests.

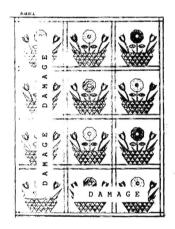 

Rebinding a severely damaged quilt can challenge one to create an ornate border to show off the remaining piece (see above). If the quilt has a decorative border and some of this border will be sacrificed in order to make whole what remains, one may frame sections from the border to pass on to other family members.

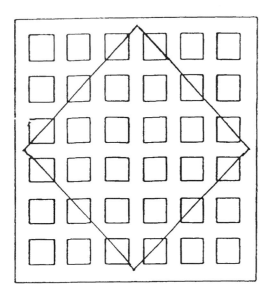

Remember to keep all sections taken off. When major damage exists on four outer edges, one may take a quilt set-in-the-square and turn it into a quilt set-in-the-diamond. Prior to doing anything, hang up the quilt and let it speak to you for anywhere from one to six months. Envision what it could be!

# Central Damage

Central damage responds to several solutions: a medallion inset, creating smaller quilts out of the original, restructuring the design.

### OPTION 1:
### *Create a medallion inset*

A Garden Maze Quilt, c. 1870, was chewed during a thunderstorm by a family's Golden Retriever. The distraught owner who loved both the quilt and the dog decided to repair the quilt and immortalize the dog by having the dog's image inserted in the central octagon. The frightened dog also destroyed two mattresses in his attempt to dig to safety. This quilt is a good example of Susan Hendrick Wilson's belief that the history of a quilt doesn't end when the quilt is completed because daily life continues to affect its condition.

When creating a new medallion inset to be framed by the existing older squares, it will be necessary to add a new backing layer of cotton

*Create a medallion inset for quilt*

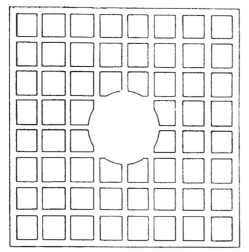 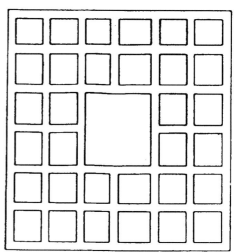

*This is the line drawing of India, the Golden Retriever Quilt Killer whose silhouette became the inset in the center octagon of the Garden Maze Quilt (above).*

If the damaged quilt is a family-owned piece and the restorer is a quilter, a hand-quilted homage to the quiltmaker makes a nice memorial to the grandmother or great grandmother whose name, place and date of birth and death can be hand quilted or appliqued into the center medallion. The book, *Old Glories,* shows two framed pictures of memorabilia that would serve as a larger medallion inset in a severely damaged quilt. Photo transfers and letters or birth and marriage certificates could be added to create a truly precious family history within the framework of the good outer squares of the family quilt. [17] A family tree with hand embroidered names and dates may also personalize such a family quilt.

Brackman points out that applique medallions were often framed with patchwork designs and patchwork designs were often framed in applique. Be free to choose your own method. If one also owns handkerchiefs or other memorabilia from the quiltmaker, one can create a Crazy Quilt collage of memories framed by the quiltmaker's handiwork.

to stabilize the weakened quilt. When inserting the new medallion you also need to re-sew the seams of the older quilt. (See Chapter III on Holes.)

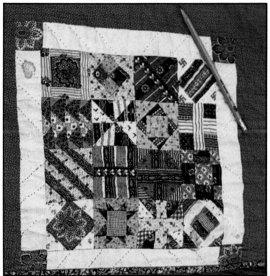

*Applique medallions were often framed with patchwork designs, and patchwork designs were often framed in applique. The quilt restorer can feel free to choose her own method.*

## OPTION 2:
### *Create one or more smaller quilts*

To create smaller quilts you begin by deciding which outer sections will be salvaged and then carefully hemrip the seams open. Cut through to the back and allow enough backing fabric for a seam allowance. Hemrip the binding away from the sections to be resewn, so that the binding can be re-applied once the sections are rebutted.

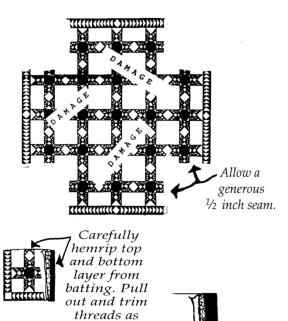

*Allow a generous ½ inch seam.*

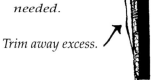

*Carefully hemrip top and bottom layer from batting. Pull out and trim threads as needed.*

*Trim away excess.*

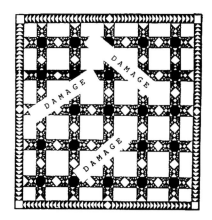

*Major central.*

*Over cut section to allow ½ inch seam allowance.*

*Completed wall quilt.*

BACK

*Sew front sections together first.*

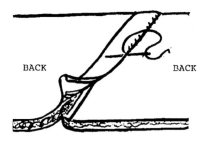

BACK          BACK

*Slip stitch back seam by hand.*

Carefully align the front sections to be resewn and resew the front sections first. Hand sewing is recommended. Older fabric has much give to it and hand sewing allows for easing of the fabric whereas machine sewing tends to create ripples.

When front sections have been resewn, turn the piece over and trim away any excess batting before resewing the back panels.

Re-apply binding which has been pinned-back and trim as needed.

Smaller quilts make whole what was tattered. As mentioned above, all extra pieces should be saved for later repairs and documentation is recommended so that the quilt's earlier condition becomes part of the quilt's history.

If a square is chosen, extra sections of the quilt may still be in good condition. These may either be framed, finished as is or incorporated into another wall hanging or small quilt.

**OPTION 3:**
*Create a quilt*

If the outer edge of a damaged quilt has nine good squares in it, the quilter may wish to re-structure these nine squares into a different setting or create a new/old quilt from the piece.

Using a quilt-as-you-go method of work-ing each square separately, the nine squares may be set on the diamond and new squares may be added using complimentary reproduc-tion fabrics. This option would require many hours but can produce stunning results.

## Erratic Damage

Erratic damage, especially on a finely executed quilt from the 1800s, burdens the heart. Drap-ing or folding it so that the damage does not

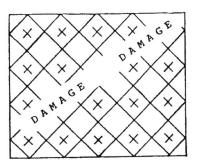

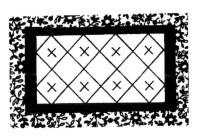

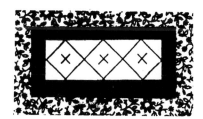

*Creative options for dealing with erratic quilts.*

Create an unusual setting to showcase four squares.

Quilt as you go method for adding sashing or border.

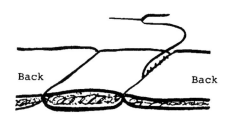

Slip stitch closed and rebuilt as desired for finishing piece..

show is the easiest and least painful way to deal with such a problem quilt.

If one must do *something* in order to make peace with the quilt, the first step is to hang it up and look at it over a period of time. What sections are still good? Can a smaller quilt be rescued out of the larger? If the quality of the quilt is so magnificent, does it merit being reassembled so that all of the good parts can be rejoined? Nancy Kirk refers to this process as "Zen and the Art of Quilt Restoration," an apt description of the meditative process involved between damaged quilts and quilt restorers. Several quilt restorers refer to this process as talking to the quilt and asking the quilt what it would like to be.

For example, can three outer good squares be donated to the central section so that one rescues a 4 x 5 section instead of a 5 x 5? Erratic damage requires that decisions are made before doing anything. Seam allowances need to be kept. The backing may need to remain whole.

A very tedious but rewarding method is to remove very carefully the severely damaged inner square and lift it out of the total quilt, so

that it can be replaced by an outer square. Once the chosen square (quilting and backing intact) is inserted into the quilt, the backing can be re-quilted onto the batting layer of the insertion.

Erratic damage is either surface damage or mouse damage. Surface damage is due to dye rot, worn fabric or poor quality fabric. Sears catalogue sold five different grades of fabric. Cheap fabric has existed forever and if the

Mouse chewed damage resembles cut snowflakes.

quiltmaker could afford only low end fabric, it wore out quickly. Whatever the reason for its disintegration, the fabric simply isn't there anymore. Surface damage is fairly easy to deal with because fabric may be inserted to replace the missing fabric. You will find specific suggestions in Chapter III on Holes.

Damage from mouse chewing is often severe and usually penetrates all of the quilt's layers. A good method to understand erratic damage due to mice, is to take a piece of paper and pretend it is a quilt. Fold the paper in half (2), in half again (4), and again (8), and again (16) and again (32).

A folded quilt usually has 16 layers, just like the folded piece of paper. Some larger quilts have 32 layers. If you cut nibbles along the folds of the paper and unfold the paper, a seemingly erratic pattern of damage appears. The same thing happens when a mouse chews a folded quilt. Generally neither scissors nor mice will penetrate the the inner folds.

Erratic quilt damage which penetrates all three layers of a quilt can be caused by decades of attic rodents stealing cotton from out of the inside. Such damage requires a large commitment of time to restore and needs to be seen as

a labor of love. (See section on "Robbing Peter to Pay Paul" in Chapter III.) Finely quilted wedding applique quilts may need actual reconstruction of the missing sections.

Erratic damage can also be dealt with by looking at the quilt as damaged fabric to be cut into usable pieces for another quilt. This method is especially good for an overall busy scrap quilt. Begin by measuring with a ruler to get the size of a square or diamond or rectangle that could be saved. Think in terms of sets of 3, 6, 9, 12, 16 and so on, and as though you were searching for tiles to set into another quilt format.

For example, if one can save nine six-inch squares from an overall disaster of a quilt, those nine squares can be set on the diamond, to create a wall hanging, or may be set on the diamond with sashing further extending the size, as shown on page 29.

In working with severe overall damage, it is best to take the time to see what the quilt can yield. Save all pieces for future repairs or use small usable pieces for tiny pillows or ornaments.

> **REMINDER:**
> DO NOT CUT UNTIL THE DESIGN TO
> BE USED IS CERTAIN

*Oak Leaf and Reel Quilt c. 1850. Red and white graphic impact of this quilt would be spectacular from afar.*

*A close-up view of the Oak Leaf and Reel Quilt at left reveals speckled damage of all the red fabric.*

## Speckled Damage

Overall damage from dye rot is irreversible. Distance is its ally. Try hanging such a quilt from a second floor stairwell, or on a high wall, and see what a spectacular impact it makes. Because the batting will fall out of each hole with laundering and use, a quilt with speckled damage should not be laundered or handled repeatedly.

The photograph of the Mariner's Compass (below) shows damage due to harsh dyes in the fabric; all of the adjoining cotton is intact. It can be dealt with by netting the circle only. This netting technique will stabilize the speckled print and still leave two-thirds of the quilt free of netting. The netting technique is only recommended if the quilt has defined areas of speckled damage and spectacular areas of hand quilting. There are other examples in Chapter VII on Victorian quilts.

*A much-loved but severely damaged Basket Quilt from the 1870s was brought by a family to the quilt clinic at the Columbia Quilt Guild show in Hillsdale, NY in 1984. In short order Kittie James Becker of K & K Quilteds made a wall hanging of it by rebutting its four corner sections. The lovely piece (above) has been hanging in the family's home ever since, giving pleasure to all.*

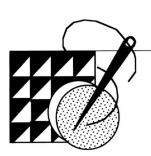

# 3

# Holes, Fading, Flaking and Applique

HOLES IN QUILTS AND CLOTHING vary in importance according to their position, their size and their fixability. Think of the difference between a hole in a pocket versus a hole in the front of a skirt.

The hole size is less important than its position. A small hole in the center of a quilt is more prominent than a large hole on the corner of a quilt. One's eye is offended by a hole in a visually prominent position. Variably-colored scrap quilts with holes are easier to repair than two- or three-color quilts with holes. Common sense says that the color should carefully match in a two- or three-color quilt.

Some holes are so predominant that they need to be seen as overall damage, as has been shown in Chapter II. If a quilt is tattered along one side or damage is located in the middle of a quilt, it may be approached as a severely damaged quilt rather than a quilt with holes. Repairing true holes in any quilt requires basic sewing techniques (see Chapter VIII), proper choice of fabric and the right method.

*Two-color quilts like this Red and White Lady of the Lake, c. 1870, are finished by tying to the back or by hand quilting. Their restoration can be complicated by the difficulty in finding exact fabric matches. Because of their many colors throughout, Album quilts such as one from 1880 (below), are pure joy to restore.*

# Surface Holes

The two most common methods used to repair holes are applique and reverse applique:

## Applique

A piece of fabric is cut ¼″ bigger than the shape to be repaired and the fabric is positioned over the shape to be recovered. The ¼″ seam allowance is folded under and precisely pinned into place. A closely matching thread is used to blind stitch or ladder stitch the fabric into place.

## Reverse Applique

All frayed or disintegrated fabric is removed in the section to be replaced. Loose threads are removed from the adjoining seams. A piece of fabric is cut ¼″ to ½″ bigger than the shape to be repaired and the fabric is tucked into and under all the adjoining seams. All the original quilt seams are carefully folded under and pinned into place. The blind stitch or ladder stitch is used to secure the patch with closely matching thread.

*Flying Geese Quilt c. 1880. Brown print triangle at front with yellow pinheads showing has been inserted into the prepared hole. See Illustrations on p. 39 for step-by-step directions.*

A tailor ham for pressing is an invaluable tool for this process. Instead of using pins that get in the way of sewing, the quilt is laid over the ham so that the hole rests on the center. The pins are inserted directly into the ham like nails into a piece of wood. Anchored in place, the patch can be sewn in half the time. (See Resources, Chapter X.)

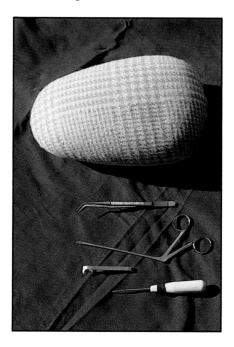

*Basic tools required in quilt restoration (from top down): Tailor ham, long tweezers, crocodile action ear polypus, wide-tipped tweezers for thread removal, and hem ripper for seams.*

Conservation methods usually require that all original fabric be left on the quilt for historical purposes. If the quilt is finely executed and merits this concern, I agree. However, many utilitarian quilts look better if the old fabric is removed and the substitute fabric is added as the only fabric layer. Restoration methods aim to repair a quilt so that "it looks as nearly as it did originally." [18] Keeping all the excess debris causes a surface puffiness that wasn't there originally. The reverse applique technique is particularly effective for sharp-tipped diamonds and triangles because all excess bulk is removed and the original fabric lies on top of the replacement fabric.

Any fabric removed from a quilt should be kept in a small bag or box and labeled for future use. Also, any repairs done on a quilt should be recorded for the family or future owner. As Susan Anderson so candidly states: "I have never received an objection from the buying public when I have pointed out any restoration I did to a quilt, as long as I used the proper fabric and noted all restorations on the price tag." [19]

## Fabric Selection: Vintage or Reproduction?

Vintage fabric is preferable to new fabric when restoring an antique quilt. However, vintage fabric is sometimes impossible to match properly. A good matching reproduction fabric may be the only solution. Hundreds of reproduction fabrics exist through the mail order outlets listed in Resources. Some are so exact in their details they can fool an expert.

By the 1870s manufacturing companies were producing thousands of prints a year in the United States alone. Add these thousands to thousands more in Europe and Asia, and you see how finding the right vintage fabric can be like looking for a needle in a haystack. Much of the calico seen in mid-19th century quilts was imported. In 1830, United States imported 3.5 yards per citizen. By the 1850s, imports had increased to 6.5 yards."

*Textile Designs* includes 1,823 color photos of some fabrics available in the last 200 years. [20] Among quilt restorers who own hundreds of thousands of pre-1930 prints, the common question is "Do you have this fabric?" To suggest that an exact match is always possible

is as misleading as telling someone she can find an exact button to match a handmade blouse purchased in Alsace-Lorraine before World War I. The fabric, like the button, may exist somewhere in the world, but finding the exact match may take a lifetime—and then some. As Shirley McElderry has said so well, "Tiger soup is easy to make, once you catch the tiger." [21]

Fortunately, an exact match of fabric design is not always as important as an exact match of tonality. If the fabric blends in with the total quilt it may work just as well. Not matching the fabric sometimes is better than matching. For example, I purchased an early 1850s Nine Patch quilt set like a single Irish Chain. Each cream square was intricately hand quilted with feathered plates. Almost all of the early chintz squares were tattered and flaking. Rather than replace the squares with early chintz, I replaced 150 squares with early 1860s indigo fabric and then re-quilted each square to imitate the triple rows of quilting. For this particular quilt, the wrong fabric was right.

Many quilts have both pleasant and unpleasant colors. Just because it was a brown piece of cloth that rotted on a multi-colored quilt, one doesn't have to replace that brown with brown. One can choose from the other colors on the quilter's palette. JoAnn Parisi, who lectures throughout the northeast on creating old-looking quilts from new fabrics, encourages her students to do what quilters have always done: piece, patch and add slight irregularity.

Vintage fabric is only a good choice if it really matches. Reproduction fabrics which match perfectly are a better choice than incorrect vintage fabric. The total impact of the quilt is more important than the authenticity of each piece of fabric. Documentation will alleviate

*Ohio Stars, made of vintage fabrics, replaced the stolen corner squares described on page 37. All extra fabric was saved and labeled for any future repairs.*

guilt and preserve the history for the next generation.

Time and money are both real concerns. If months or years of searching for the perfect vintage fabric has not led to a find, then a good reproduction fabric may be the solution. Many fabric manufacturers consciously imitate older designs and colors just as manufacturers did centuries ago. [22] Imitation of the old always existed and nostalgia reigned throughout the latter part of the 19th century into the early 20th.

## *Scrap Quilts: A Joy*

Scrap quilts, as previously noted, are a joy to restore because the fabrics are chosen to blend into the totality of as many as a hundred or more colors. Light or dark shades are usually the main concern in matching fabric to a scrap quilt. To see if the fabric will blend with the totality, pin the fabric to the damaged section, and then hang or drape the quilt so that you can step back and study it for a while.

A mirror is a wonderful household tool for adding distance to your view within a smaller room. Hang or drape the quilt, walk as far away as possible, and turn your back on the quilt while holding a small wall mirror or mirror tile in your hand. The reflected image of the quilt will tell you whether the fabric blends into the quilt or not. Margaret Bricker suggests using binoculars backwards "to give you a distance perspective and help you decide what to add and where." (See Spears article, p. 50) Polaroid pictures also reduce nicely!

*Bear Paw Fabrics are old and new (1880s to 1991). Created for a specific wall, this Bear Paw aims to re-create the look of an old quilt in colors compatible with the client's decor.*

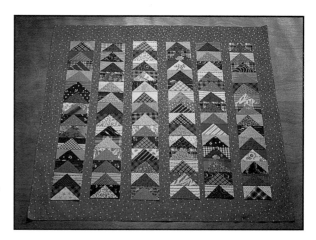

*Reproduction fabrics rest at peace with vintage fabrics in this restoration. Some reproduction fabric may actually look older than the original vintage.*

## Two- or Three-Color Quilts: Robbing Peter to Pay Paul

Difficult to match for exact color, two- or three-color quilts often require that fabric be stolen from a less visible section in order to repair a hole in a more prominent section. A border may be trimmed on one side to give the restorer enough fabric to repair the hole. Fabric may be taken from corner blocks in order to repair central blocks.

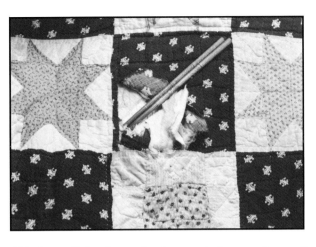

*Ohio Star quilt has damage in a large central square. Because the eye rests on the center of the quilt, whether on a bed or a wall, such damage requires careful repair (see below).*

*Note discoloration on outer border and two sashing strips of this Ohio Star Quilt. One complete outer border was removed and used full width to repair sashing. All borders were then trimmed back to exactly half their original size.*

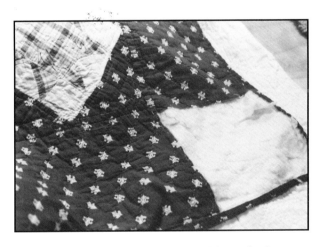

*The replacement fabric came from the quilt's own border, a distinctive French blue fabric that may have been imported. Two corner blocks were used to repair center damage.*

*Taking from the corner squares to give to the center damage is often the most practical way to find the just-right fabric, especially when the original quilt is a hundred years old, worn and faded.*

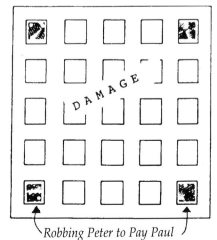

*Robbing Peter to Pay Paul*

Quilts will often have a vanity block, which the restorer may wish to create on a corner in order to fix a central hole. Quilts often have two or four different corner blocks. Keep in mind that this method of stealing from the quilt to give back to the quilt is very time consuming. It takes three to four times as long as a straightforward replacement. Patience to carefully hemrip all the fabric is needed; however, the quilt is aesthetically more pleasing in the end.

Stealing fabric from the quilt in order to give it back is truly one of the most economical and aesthetically pure forms of restoring. This method is more time consuming because it requires preparing two or more sections and restoring two or more sections.

Hand applique quilts usually have needed fabric hidden beneath the applique design. To get at this fabric requires that the applique stitches be removed. This method is particular-

*Pineapple Applique Quilt c. 1870. Pineapple design has been reproduced on paper pattern and green fabric is being prepared for application. Note the orange fabric hidden underneath the green fabric. Every applique hides some fabric underneath its design. Although it's tedious work, one can carefully lift the top applique to steal from the fabric beneath.*

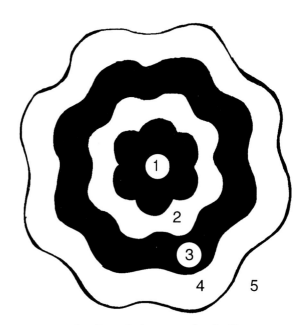

*Applique designs are often built up layer-upon-layer of fabric.*

Fabric **#5** is under fabric **#4**

Fabric **#4** is under fabric **#3**

Fabric **#3** is under fabric **#2**

Fabric **#2** is under fabric **#1**

ly helpful when small holes are in need of an exact match. Borders, backing and outside blocks may all be seen as sources of fabric for restoring the inner section of a quilt.

## False Re-quilting: Finishing Step

When a hole exists in a quilted area and when the replacement fabric is sewn in place, the new section needs to be re-quilted so that the quilting pattern remains constant and the replacement piece disappears within the quilting pattern. If the quilting design is complex, a piece of plastic or tissue paper may be used to draw the exact quilting pattern prior to replacing the damaged section.

If the original quilting was crude, the re-quilting should also be. Utilitarian quilts often have five stitches or fewer per inch. If fine, tiny quilting stitches were used, then the re-quilting should be just as finely sewn.

Once the section has been carefully reconstructed, a closely matching quilting thread should be prepared as if for hand quilting. Pop your knot as you would for regular quilting, and manipulate the fabric and batting to create the quilting design without letting the threaded needle penetrate into the back layer. This method of false quilting is easier to accomplish than it sounds. If the process frightens you, practice without knotting your thread to get the feel of quilting on the top two layers only. By using this method, the quilting design on the back of the quilt remains exactly as it began.

## Hole Size

The *Needlecraft Encyclopedia* tells the reader to cut the hole into a square or rectangle prior to

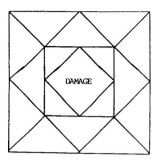

*Remove all damaged fabric.*

*Remove all dangling threads from seam allowance.*

*Insert batting if needed.*

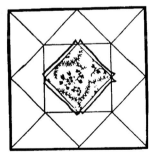

*Insert chosen fabric as if inserting within a picture frame.*

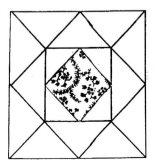

*Turn under ¼" seam allowance from quilt and sew carefully so that stitches do not show. Ladder stitch or blind hem stitch.*

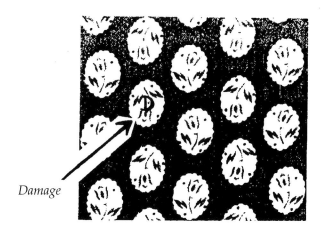

*If one small section is torn on a print with a bold pattern, often a small repair using reverse applique in a compatible fabric will blend into the totality of the busy print.*

mending or patching. When working within the framework of a quilt, which has its own design, the quilt design should guide the restorer.

If the hole is in a triangle or hexagon, it is best to replace the entire damaged shape. This solution means that a bigger shape is a better choice to hide the effect of the repair.

If the hole is in a very busy print, often a small hole may be repaired using reverse applique. For example, if the fabric is a 1930s print of peach, blue and white, a small piece of peach or blue or white may be inserted into the hole the way one inserts a picture within a picture frame, and the 1930s fabric may be slightly clipped and turned under for close blind stitching. Busy prints work very well with this method.

If the hole is in a sashing section, it may be best to recreate the entire section of the sashing. If this is not possible, a smaller square or rectangle the size of the sashing may be created so that the sashed section looks pieced by the quiltmaker. Pieced sashing was commonly seen in utilitarian quilts and is not usually offensive to the eye.

The grain of the replacement fabric

should match the grain of its surrounding fabric whenever possible. The direction of the print or design should also match the direction of the surrounding fabric. Remember that the restorer's goal is to have the replacement piece blend into the totality of the quilt.

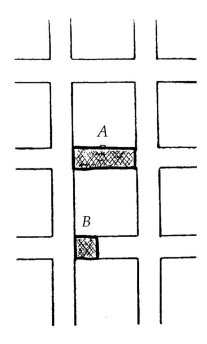

*A square or rectangular replacement is less offensive to the eye.*

*(A)*
*A rectangle is first choice.*

*(B)*
*Square may be necessary if the sashing is hard to match and must be taken from the side of the quilt.*

## Cereal Bowl Holes

Quilt squares may have major damage the size of cereal bowls or even platters. Fillings for large holes may be recreated first and then inset within the prepared frame. Any error in piecing can be adjusted on the smaller pieced section prior to insertion within the square, diamond, triangle or whatever shape fits the reconstruction of the quilt. Once the large section, panel or row is recreated, it is inserted within the waiting quilt as if it were a simple patch.

In order to create the exact size needed, make a template using plastic or tracing paper to outline the design needed and add the ¼" for sewing. Sew all the pieces as if sewing a block from the quilt and then inset the section as if it were an ordinary patch following the illustrations here.

Below is a breakdown of possible sections which may be damaged. Pretend that each of these sections represents a damaged section and needs to be recreated in the quilt.

A square made up of two or four triangles is easier to inset and takes less sewing time.

A machine pieced ring of hexagons is easier to inset than each individual hexagon.

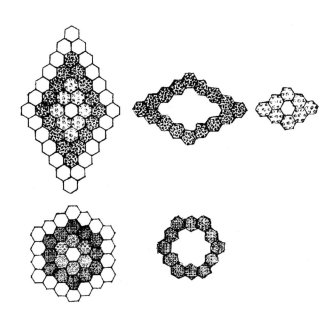

A quadrant of a Fan or Dresden Plate is easier to inset than individual wedges.

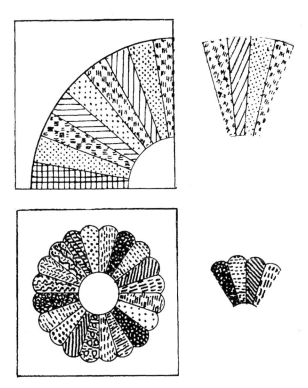

Rows are easier to inset and blend into the totality of the restoration than a multitude of smaller sections.

Think in terms of shapes to inset when recreating major damage in a quilt. The more that you can create on a sewing machine and the larger area of damage you can cover with the prepared piece, the faster and easier the repair.

# Fading Fabric

Fabric that has faded for 30, 50 or 100 years is not the same shade as new fabric—even if it is the exact print and vintage. Laundering and drying in the sun can speed up the aging process. New fabric may also be left in a sunny spot, outside or inside, so that a week or a month may produce the lighter shade. One month is usually the most time needed for direct sunlight to effectively fade vintage fabric.

Fading kits are available which also work well at both fading and tendering fabric. Shirley McElderry has had wonderful success using the fading kits and recommended them in an article in *American Quilter.* [23] Patience is needed to get the feel of using fade kits; I recommend experimenting on various unimportant fabrics first so that you don't repeat the mistake I once made in using a fading kit on real vintage fabric. (Resources)

Reversing a fabric can sometimes achieve the same effect as fading. Often the backside of the print is more muted and resembles the aged look on the quilt. Experiment with shades that may have the same colors and turn them all to the wrong side. One vintage black print with tiny white flowers that looked too new on the right side was perfect on the wrong side. Experiment, pin, walk away and look in the mirror, use the binoculars or take a Polaroid picture.

## Custom Dyeing

If a whole cloth quilt requires a perfect shade for matching there are textile specialists who can custom dye 100% cotton fabric to match the needed color. Often an older vintage cotton sheet may be used and sent with the color specification. This solution is best for larger areas that need to be reworked. (Resources)

## Tea Dyeing

Tea dying has been used by many quilters to give an aged, faded look to bright cottons. Lightly used, it can be very effective. Refer to articles on natural dyes. Some quilters strongly believe that the tannic acid in the tea can be harmful to the fabric; on the other hand, Barbara Brackman notes that a few fabrics in the Baltimore Album quilts were tea dyed. Several quilters prefer to use commercial dye such as Rit tan dye, and still others make their own dyes from natural plants to achieve a less new look.

# Holes in the Whole Cloth

Holes in white quilted areas require a sensitive look at the existing quilting design. If a hole exists in a feather or two of a Feathered Plate quilting design, it is best to applique an exact replica of the feather and embed the stitches on the quilting line.

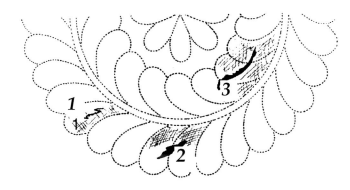

*(1)*
*Recreate one feather and applique over quilting line to simulate quilting stitch.*

*(2)*
*Recreate two feathers and follow the same procedure as one, but add requilting between the two feathers.*

*(3)*
*Recreate three feathers and repeat all the same.*

*Damage in a quilted area is less noticeable if the repair simulates the quilting design and is embedded within the lines of the design. A perforated template may need to be created in order to reproduce the exact design on the applique repair.*

Using a plastic sheet, outline the damaged section within the quilting lines with a fine Sharpie or with a pencil on tracing paper. Add ¼" for turning under and applique the piece onto the section as if it were a traditional applique.

Darning and mending can be effectively used by placing a piece of fabric under the hole and carefully following the directions in "Sewing Techniques Review" (Chapter VIII). The trick to effective darning or mending is to take miniscule stitches that disappear within the grain of the fabric. The direction of the stitches must closely parallel the direction of the weave in order to blend in perfectly. Some quilts have been so finely repaired in the early part of this century that the repairs are almost invisible today.

## Major Holes

A major hole is repaired in the same way as a small hole. Think of the three layers of a quilt with a top, middle and back. A major hole requires reconstruction of the top and of the bottom and filler in between. The methods described above are applied to repairing a hole that penetrates all three layers of a quilt. Applique a square or rectangular piece of matching fabric to the back of the quilt and then turn the quilt right side up. Add a layer of batting made of the existing filling—cotton, wool, flannel, polyester, sheeting—and insert the appropriate fabric on the front of the quilt. Pin in place as directed above, sew and re-quilt as needed.

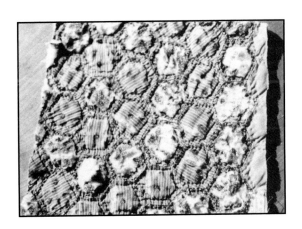

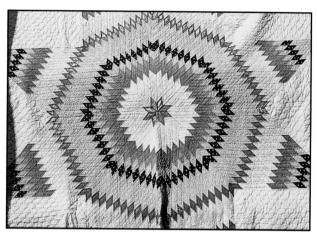

*Lone Star Quilt c. 1860. Every red diamond on the outer edge had self-destructed on this family-owned quilt. New red cotton was custom dyed and the owner is meticulously restoring the Lone Star to its original beauty.*

# Flaking Damage

Here are examples of flaking damage. Harsh dyes have destroyed the cotton fibers throughout the Honeycomb quilt fragment from the 1870s (page 43). Fragile weighted silk crumples like dry autumn leaves. Massive cracking throughout the Baby Block quilt (above) makes it impossible to repair.

Flaking quilts should not be handled, because each handling causes more disintegration of brittle or powdery fabric. As framed display pieces however, they can gain a new life. The fusing methods described in Chapter VII, Victorian Quilts, are most effective for stabilizing flaking damage.

Some restorers of Crazy Quilts recommend netting. However, netting does not stop silk from flaking. Indeed, the netting can turn into pouch-like receptacles that hold the silk debris. If a flaking quilt will be used exclusively as an art piece, fusing the fabric is a preferred alternative.

# Applique Quilts

Applique designs may be reproduced using the traditional applique methods illustrated in all general quilting books. Most often applique designs are applied by either needle turning the ¼" seam allowance, or by drawing the design on freezer paper and ironing the ¼" seam allowance over the paper..

## Self-Turned Applique Design

A wonderful trick which can be used in any applique is a sew, cut and turn method which requires two layers of fabric. Draw the desired shape to the exact size. Cut out the paper or plastic template to the exact size. Do not add a seam allowance.

If the desired shape is a leaf, cut out two pieces of fabric ½" larger than the desired leaf size. Cut the fabric so that the grain and design match the quilt's design.

Place the fabric's good sides together as if to be sewn on a machine. Outline the template exactly onto the wrong side of the fabric. Use a sharpened pencil for light fabric or soapstone for dark fabric. The exact outline is machine sewn with stitch length at 1 on most machines which makes tiny, close stitches.

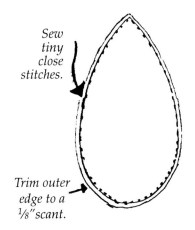

*Sew tiny close stitches.*

*Trim outer edge to a ⅛"scant.*

Trim away excess fabric to ⅛" to ¹⁄₁₆" all around the design.

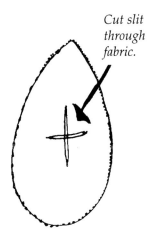

*Cut slit through fabric.*

Lift the top layer of the sewn fabric—that is the layer the exact design was drawn on. A quilting pin or stiletto will lift the fabric. Once it's lifted, you can cut a line in the middle of the top layer.

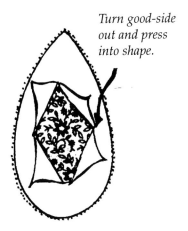

*Turn good-side out and press into shape.*

Turn the piece so that the good side of the fabric is on the outside. Gently extend the fabric along the sew line and press the design so that the sew line does not show. Applique the leaf in place using traditional applique methods.

*Applique ready for sewing.*

This draw, sew, cut and turn method may be used to reconstruct any design and is one of the most versatile tricks to control the desired shape of the applique. A square or diamond may be reproduced as easily as a heart or tulip. The shape of the design does not matter because the method will work with any needed applique.

Prior to using this method on vintage fabric, experiment by making simple shapes to get the feel of creating a self-turned applique. If the backing fabric seems too bulky for the particular quilt, excess fabric may be trimmed away from the cut back fabric as desired.

Any thin fabric works very well for the second layer and a shoe box of light and dark fabric shades may be kept exclusively for this purpose. Most fabric stores sell lightweight liner fabrics and baby fabrics that are excellent for controlling the shape without adding bulk.

Sunbonnet Sue may be recreated in this fashion just as easily as a Rose of Sharon. All layers may be built up in this same way. The self-turned applique can be used for people, buildings, trees, flower petals and three-dimensional leaves. Goddu uses the method in her construction of pictorial scenes, referring to it as a double-sided faced unit. [24] Helma Stewart uses a similar method to create three-dimensional flowers such as those seen on Victorian Crazy Quilts. [25] Once a few of these "patches" are recreated, this method may turn out to be the preferred method for preparing most Victorian wedges as well as traditional diamonds and triangles which can be very difficult to needle turn. The close trimming of sharp corners eliminates all the bulk which frequently creates a problem.

All appliques are sewn by imitating the method used on each individual quilt. If the original quiltmaker appliqued a red flower with white thread, then white thread and the same stitches should be reproduced on the new appliqued section. If the quilter used red thread, then red thread should be used.

Applique butterflies, umbrellas and Sunbonnet Sues were traditionally appliqued with the buttonhole stitch with dark embroidery floss. (See Chapter VIII for more on hand sewing.)

*Chopstick indicates damage of cotton to be replaced by hemripping and lifting applique leaves and heart. After a matching cotton fabric is inserted, the leaves and heart will be re-appliqued to thier new resting place.*

## Damage to the Applique Background Fabric

When severe damage exists to the background fabric onto which an applique design is sewn, it may be necessary to repair the cream, white or muslin fabric. First decide how large a section needs to be replaced. As in a traditional pieced quilt, a larger repair is often a better choice than many small repairs.

Once the circle, quadrant, or rectangle has been decided upon, then all the applique sections which rest on this section must have their stitching removed so that the damaged fabric can be removed and the replacement fabric inset below.

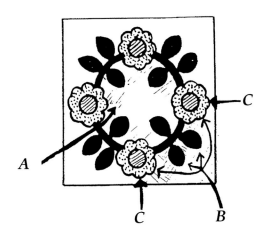

### (A)

*Inner damage in the center of an applique may require removing the applique stitches from all the central leaves and flowers so that a new circle of fabric may be replaced and all the leaves and flowers re-appliqued.*

### (B)

*Outer damage may require that a large section of cotton fabric is replaced by removing the stitches on the leaves and flowers in the outer quadrant of the applique block.*

### (C)

*Adding a quadrant section of cotton fabric from points C to C will minimize the visual impact of the repair.*

The irregularity of freehand applique designs makes them easy to modify in order to repair any damage. In the beautiful museum-quality quilt shown below, the irregularity of the exquisite detail extends throughout the border. Many early quiltmakers improvised as they went along. If an error was made, they adjusted accordingly and simply kept on going.

*Red and white applique quilt c. 1890. This cut-out square made with reverse applique appears <u>only</u> <u>once</u> on the entire quilt. Did the quiltmaker snip her own fabric by mistake and decide to turn it into reverse applique?*

*Finely appliqued, these amoebic shapes have a certain primitive folk charm. The quilter, who obviously enjoyed applique work, completed a king size quilt! Wrong or right may not be an issue in many quilts. That they are still with us attests to the quiltmaker's determination to create something whole from pieces of fabric.*

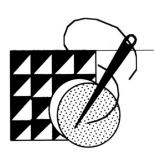

# 4

# Ugly Ducklings:
# One Step from the Landfill

BAGS OF WHAT WE CALL "orphan quilts" are often left on the doorstep at K & K Quilteds. Names are never attached. No one wants to claim them. Like foundlings from a half century before, they are discarded by their owners.

Not all damaged quilts are beautiful; not all were beautiful when they were made. For centuries, women have been expected to provide warm covers for their families. This domestic imperative did not necessarily give the quiltmaker the ability or the fabric to make good quilts. Some quilts are so ugly and badly made one wonders if the quiltmaker was deliberately protesting her subjugation. Erratic quilts and tops with chopped-off points in rambling rows with crooked piecing speak of poverty, necessity and disdain for the process.

Some quilt tops are so disheveled and grotesque as to suggest yet other causes. When I find seams sewn backwards, inside out and upside down, with raw edges to the front, I remember that these quilts were sewn in days when women innocently ordered some now-outlawed products from the 1897 Sears catalogue: 4-ounce bottles of laudanum opium for 29 cents [26] and cocaine-laced snuff used by women "all over the country, at all levels of society, by young and old." [27] I have a picture from an 1885 advertisement that shows a woman smoking a cocarette, made of Bolivian coca leaves and Virginia tobacco, and gives 10 reasons for choosing this product. Reason 6 claims "Coca is the finest nerve tonic and exhilarator ever discovered" and reason 8 says

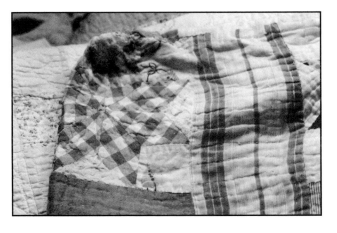

"Coca stimulates the brain to great activity and gives tone and vigor to the entire system". Once I came upon an 1887 trade card for Mrs. Winslow's Soothing Syrup, an opium-laced syrup for "colicky and nervous" children. [28] One wonders about women who used these products unwittingly and never thought about addiction because no one knew of the dark side of these enticingly advertised products.

Yes, there are ugly quilts that are thrown away because they produce shudders of horror to anyone who sees them in their totality. Inherited or purchased, these ugly ducklings challenge that kindly spirit that wants to save handmade work. Disregarding all rules of symmetry, balance and color, such quilts can have great charm when used in moderation. Saving a 40" square from an 80" monster can be a practical and praiseworthy salvage.

Cutting quilts brings a horror of amputation. Guilt of violating a whole object and of violating the quiltmaker are very strong emotions in most quilters and quilt owners. Hawaiian quiltmakers in the 1800s believed so strongly that the quiltmaker's spirit or "mana" was contained within the quilt, that many early Hawaiian quilts were burned on the funeral pyre so that the quilter's spirit would be free to pursue an afterlife. This Hawaiian belief is reflected in some of our modern-day feeling about quilts.

Our guilt can be absolved when we think of gardeners. Gardeners weed their gardens; they thin out plants so that others may prosper and they easily throw rotten vegetables on compost heaps. Trees are pruned regularly to enhance the growth of the whole. Harvest always includes separating the good from the bad. If a neighbor brings a basket of tomatoes, the basket is sorted immediately to protect the good from the rotten. We prune, we thin and

protect natural growth; we clean and discard the non-usable. We think nothing of using a cut-down dining table as a coffee table, or a treadle sewing machine as a table base. We praise ourselves for framing grandma's doily. We replace broken ring stones. We restyle wedding dresses.

Ugly duckling quilts, in need of transformation, wish to be true beauties. When a totally grotesque Nine Patch was brought to the studio, we saw a common denominator of red and blue indigo, but its ballooning top was unmanageable. It was made from fabric from 1880–1900 and had been pieced sporadically over 20 years. Hand piecing, done in times of peacefulness or exhaustion, often explains undulating waves in a quilt top. The poofiness can never be made to lie flat, short of taking apart the stitches and re-stitching the entire piece. Jeannie Spears took on such a project which required three years of spare time to take apart and three years of spare time to reassemble properly. [29] Such a labor of love requires heartfelt perseverance in even the most determined restorer.

Unlike the magnificent quilt top Jeannie Spears restored to splendor, the grotesque Nine Patch brought to us needed to be reined in. By reducing its overwhelming array into a 50" square and by framing the square within a double border of blue followed by a red border, this busy quilt top was made to sparkle quietly within its new frame. I like to think that the anonymous maker is smiling in approval. Made for utility, a quilt top or finished quilt can become an art piece to be enjoyed for decades to come. I personally would cherish such immortality. When approached with kindness and artistic vision, even the ugliest of ducklings can be transformed into swans.

A few years ago, a family-owned quilt was

laid across the studio table by an older couple whose eyes revealed the hopelessness they felt. Unable to discard this much-loved quilt, they wished to know if anything could be done with the remnants. Two sections were chosen for transformation into wall hangings. Three more sections with added borders were selected for framing. For 15 years, this couple had owned a family quilt that looked like a rag. Tattered, torn and stained, it no longer served its quilt purpose. Transformed into wall hangings and framed art pieces, however, it regained new life to be enjoyed by all family members. "You do what the old quiltmakers did," said the husband with enthusiasm. "You take something that no longer has purpose in one function and transform it into another."

When a quilt's sentimental value far exceeds its monetary value, the quilt owner must ask which choice will best preserve the remaining pieces of the family's quilt heritage. Keeping a ragged quilt in a closet because one cannot bear to look at it does nothing to preserve the quiltmaker's memory. Reclaiming smaller sections which can be rescued from a severely damaged quilt, the owner regains enjoyment of the family's heritage and can pass on a legacy of love for decades to come.

# Crooked Quilts

Crooked or off-center quilts exist because the quiltmaker simply made the quilt to fit the bed or the backing and did not care that the overall design went askew. Like old colonial houses that were built by eye rather than measurement, many quilts have make-fit pieces that serve to make the quilt bigger. Crooked quilts don't look crooked on a bed because the borders or added sections usually drape down the sides. Many quilts which are somewhat wacky have a charming folk art quality to them. Hung on a wall, some look off-center and create an annoyance in the same way that a crooked picture frame demands straightening. Others can look stunningly graphic.

*BELIEVE IT OR NOT, SOME QUILTS ARE WORSE THAN THIS!*

How can you tell whether a crooked quilt will come off looking stunning? Cosmetic alignment is the answer. Decide where the true center is on the quilt. Measure out from this center to decide where it should end or could end. Mark with pins and hang it up on a wall. Stand back from the quilt to truly see it. An effective trick to add distance is to use a mirror and turn your back to the quilt. In the mirror reflection, the quilt appears twice the distance away. A Polaroid picture of it can also help because it reduces a large visual field to a smaller concentrated format. Seeing a quilt from a distance or reduced to a 3" square picture, allows the quilt to define itself.

Ask questions. Does it need a frame? If so, what color should the frame be? What width should the frame be? Would the design have more movement without a frame? Ask children; ask adult friends. Often other viewers repeat the same opinion differently. Remember, the crooked quilt has been in this condition for a long time and there is no need to rush into a solution.

I often hang up a problem quilt and ask it to tell me what it wants me to do. I live with it a while to give it time to speak to me. Sculptors talk to their stone; carvers talk to their wood. They allow themselves the time to discover what the stone or wood wants to be. Quilts do the same thing if we let them. Other possible rehabilitations for crooked and off-center quilts are found ahead in Chapter V on borders and bindings.

The Cocarettes advertisment not only features the picture of a young women smoking, but also lists ten reasons which make this addictive product desirable for the consumer. Without our present - day knowledge of cocaine, these products were seen by the innocent consumer as beneficial.

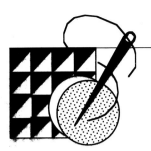

# 5

# Borders and Bindings

"A properly designed border, in the right color scheme, once again draws an eye to the important part of the quilt, its pattern." [30]

TO TRULY UNDERSTAND the powerful impact of both borders and bindings, make a field trip to a frame shop. A half hour gives you enough time to recognize the importance of both framing and matting an art piece. Quilts can be enhanced by their borders and bindings just as paintings or prints are enhanced by their mats and frames.

Quilts from necessity, however, often have borders and bindings made of leftover fabrics that bear no relationship to the quilt itself. Most borders and bindings are utilitarian and functional rather than artistically essential to the finished quilt. You get the idea if you think of a quilt as a house and the border or binding as a fence that defines the perimeter of the house's lot. Borders and bindings can either enhance or detract from a quilt. This is not opinion; this is factual in the same way that a fence either enhances or detracts from a house. A chain link fence would be inappropriate for a log cabin home, just as a split rail fence would be to a Greek Revival Mansion.

*1930s Pumpkin Orange was added to an 1890s Indigo and White Quilt. This multi-generational quilt shows quilt restoration at its worst. The present owner decided NOT to live with this added pumpkin orange border. A wise decision!*

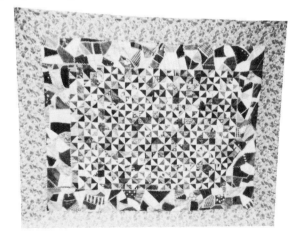

*Psychedelic Rayon from the 1930s was added to an 1880s Crazy Quilt which was obviously finished by a quilter who hand quilted her 10-inch added border of rayon. Note that the original Crazy Quilt maker had already bordered her own quilt which apparently wasn't enough for the later quiltmaker who no doubt intended it for bed use. The present quilt owner decided to return the Victorian Crazy Quilt to the original quiltmaker's intent and eliminated the rayon border and rebound the edge in black velvet.*

The foregoing photos are classic examples of earlier quilt tampering or quilt restoration. Someone found a quilt top and used fabric on hand to finish it and extend its size. To live with the badly finished quilt requires that we give the 1930 quilter the right to define what the earlier quilt will be. Many quilts that have problem borders and bindings were tampered with by a second or third quilter, or quilt owner. A good example of this tampering or previous restoration is an 1880s Hourglass in dark browns with orange madder prints. It was bordered with pastel pink from the 1930s and then hand tied. When found in a thrift shop, this quilt had a chartreuse polyester binding which only magnified the previous desecration of the original quilt.

To keep a quilt in its "found" condition, is often a disservice to the original quiltmaker. Many quilts from the 1840s to the 1930s have suffered through many owners who did what they wished to finish or preserve the quilt. To keep 50 years of poor choices permanently affixed to an antique quilt is like keeping eight layers of white paint on hand carved mahogany molding.

# When To Change Borders and How

Any quilt can be bordered or not bordered. If a border enhances the overall effect of a quilt and is aesthetically pleasing, then it should remain. However, if a quilt border overwhelms or violates the inner quilt, its validity needs to be questioned. Because quilts were made to fit beds, borders were often created to make the quilt top large enough to fit the desired bed. As bed quilts they are to be enjoyed as is, but as wall quilts they often need to be trimmed. Here follow eight different ways of dealing with borders:

*NO BORDER **LONE STAR** QUILT*

*When a quilt with no border is placed on a white wall, the quilt tends to blend into the background. Often a narrow border can contain the graphic impact of such a quilt. On the other hand, a quilt with no border on a dark wall can expand its impact in such a way that the wall itself becomes its frame.*

**OPTION 1:**
## No Border

Many a quilt has no border and the overall quilt design merely ends with the binding off of the raw edges. The no-border finish is particularly effective with an overall graphic design such as Log Cabin, Baby Block or Honeycomb. The original quiltmaker may have created a top large enough for its purpose and felt no need to add this extra step.

Any quilt with a problem border—clashing fabric from another era, badly deteriorated edges, major discoloration due to poor fabric—

may be enhanced by removing the border. Deciding to remove a border places the quilt in a large category of borderless quilts.

## OPTION 2:
### *Oversized Border to be Trimmed*

*OVERSIZED BORDER TO BE TRIMMED*

Quilts with oversized borders were usually finished to fit particular beds and the borders were made from the same fabric as the pieced or appliqued sections of the quilt. However, many oversized borders appear in clashing colors or fabrics from a much later time. If the quilt top and its border have absolutely no relationship to each other, the eye mandates that the border be removed or trimmed down so that the original quilt design can breathe.

Oversized borders, whether in original fabric or later fabric, tend to overwhelm the quilt design when the quilt is displayed on a wall. One would not put a six-inch photo into a

24-inch frame because the tiny photo would be overpowered. Likewise, an oversized border detracts from the original quilt design.

An effective way to decide how much of the border to remove is to fold under and baste (or safety pin) the layers together so that only the narrower border shows. If one feels strongly that the border should not be cut, one can effectively baste the folded-under section so that it remains on the quilt without overpowering its graphic impact when hung on a wall. If one chooses to fold under and baste, one can create a sleeve for hanging at the same time by folding under the sides first and leaving open the sides of the top and bottom for a rod.

*TRIMMED BORDER*

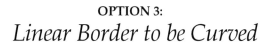

*LINEAR BORDER TO BE CURVED*

*LINEAR BORDER TO BE CURVED OR TRIMMED*

*Arrows indicate direction for measuring.
Most borders are irregular in finished size, due to
quiltmaker or laundering.*

### OPTION 3:
## Linear Border to be Curved

Often a curved edge quilt design was finished off by sewing the curved edge onto a straight grained and oversized fabric. This solution was no doubt aimed at fitting the bed. Most often seen with Double Wedding Rings and Grandmother's Flower Gardens, these large solid fabric bands often detract from the delicacy of the overall design. Most often, these oversized borders are seen on summer spreads; not wishing to give the piece more time than it was worth, the finisher simply appliqued the top to another piece of fabric for a quick extension of its size.

Using a 12-inch ruler, one can simulate the curved edge of the quilt design, so that the finished border will blend in with the curvilinear motif. If one does not wish to curve the entire border, one can still minimize its overwhelming impact by trimming part of it, so that the curved edges create a swag border effect.

### OPTION 4:
## Oversized Borders That Become Double Borders

If an oversized border competes too strongly with the quilt design because of its color and design, one may wish to create a double border. For example, if a seaweed pink fabric was used to create an 18-inch border on a brown and pink quilt, one could add a nine-inch border of brown to double frame the entire quilt.

Double borders, like double mats on a painting, pull both colors out of the design to be enhanced. Often, a single-color oversized border in a two-or three-color quilt demands that the border color becomes the predominant color seen. By laying strips of fabric over the large border–framing out the border–one can see the effect created. Multi-colored quilts often have several predominant colors, and they can literally be made to sparkle when a second border color is added.

*OVERSIZED BORDERS THAT BECOME
DOUBLE OR TRIPLE BORDERS*

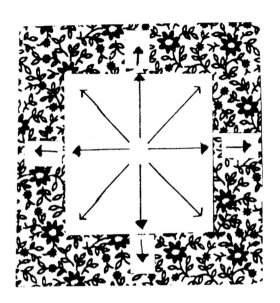

*MEASURE BORDERS FROM CENTER*

A most effective way to minimize the effect of an oversized border is to create a band of fabric which will visually divide the oversized border into three sections. The band can be easily created by sewing up a tube of fabric to the desired width. The tube is ironed flat with the seam in the middle and then appliqued onto the border. The band may be appliqued so that both sides are even or it may be appliqued so that the first band of the existing border is the same size as the band. Once appliqued, the band needs to be re-quilted to make it blend with the entire border.

Before appliqueing a straight length of fabric to an oversized border or a tube-like band of fabric to the middle of a border, use a 12" ruler to mark off the exact placement of the additional band. Always work from the center of the quilt out to the sides.

Oversized borders which appear to be the same size really are not. If any adjustments need to be made, they can be made to the outer edge.

If the original border was mitered, the bands should be mitered; if the original border was simply squared off, then the bands should be applied to imitate the original border.

### OPTION 5:
## *Erratic Borders and Crooked Quilts*

Many quilts have borders that were diagonally trimmed so that they resemble pie shaped wedges. Again the quilt was trimmed to fit the backing and batting as a functional bed cover. Sometimes these wacky borders work and add a folk art charm to the overall design. Other times these make-do wedges suggest that a later quilter finished an earlier quilt top and did it badly. If a finely designed and executed quilt is finished off poorly, you can guess that the original quilt top was violated at a later date.

To live with someone else's mistakes seems a bit silly when one can return the original quilt top to its earlier condition. Poor finishing by a second or third owner is just that. All of the options can be considered in dealing with it.

## OPTION 6:
# Inappropriate and Unusual Borders

Necessity forced many quilters to finish quilts with inappropriate borders. Whether the original quiltmaker or a later quiltmaker added a grotesquely clashing fabric to border a pleasing quilt top, the effect is the same. If the border just doesn't look right, any of the above listed options can be used.

Remember the earlier image of the chain link fence surrounding an otherwise pleasing house? Borders are like fences and can be removed without violating the integrity of the quilt top design.

Unusual borders are often added for playful reasons or for showpiece finishing. If a quilt has an unusual finish–such as ruffles, fringe, prairie points, ruching or petals–this indicates that the quiltmaker invested long hours of time. Removing fanciful borders is not advised because quilts can be highly valued for their odd finishings alone by both collectors and museums. Collectors, textile conservators and museum curators are more likely to accept the damage in order to save the quilt's peculiarity.

Quilt lovers, quilters and decorators are all more likely to take offense at a tattered or rotted border and reject it no matter how intricate a design the quiltmaker created. Again, common sense is the golden rule. One, two or

*Red and White Quilt c. 1850. Unusual quilt border reflects age. Note paper triangle which clearly shows the cut sawtooth design which was meticulously hand-appliqued along two sides of the outer border. This deceptively simple-looking border is a rare example of an appliqued sawtooth which predates the more common pieced sawtooth border.*

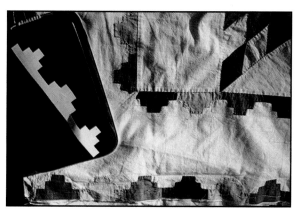

*Blazing Star Quilt, pieced and appliqued c. 1860. Note un-usual border on the paper cut-out of simulated Log Cabin rectangles. This border is hand appliqued and predates the pieced Log Cabin. At first glance the border appears simple; however, the method of construction makes this quilt top an historical artifact.*

four sides may be eliminated if the damage warrants. Two- and three-sided borders are all so common that to eliminate one or two sides can greatly improve the overall look of a quilt. If all the edges are badly damaged then a complete removal may be necessary.

If there are any somewhat good sections left on the panels being removed, keep them in a box to repair any future damage on the quilt.

Mark what the bag or box contains so that at some later time pieces are not thrown out as scraps. We have heard too many stories about old quilts and coverlets which went to the dump because the main part or sides were severely damaged.

Modifications can sometimes be created so that part of the original border remains in a scallop or swag and adds a graceful and elegant look to the entire quilt. A smaller section to be enjoyed is preferable to a larger section to be neglected and ignored. I always ally myself with the quiltmaker who prefers appreciation to neglect.

## OPTION 7:
## *Piping*

Pre-Civil War quilts often have borders that include narrow piped edges. The miniscule piping adds a dramatic impact to the border. Again, this narrow band of contrasting color works like a narrow mat under a large mat in a framed painting. If a border needs replacement, consider using a narrow row of piping if it is a pre-Civil War quilt. This finish is particularly effective on red, green and yellow applique wedding quilts because the second or third color used in the piping integrates the colors used in the appliqued quilt.

Fabric strips are cut to ¾" and string or yarn may be used to add the slight amount of bulk needed to achieve this effect.

STRING OR YARN

## OPTION 8:
## *Adding a Border*

Borders can be added to quilt tops today, just as borders were added to quilt tops in decades

past. Unlike the quilters of earlier centuries, present-day quilters have access to hundreds of reproduction fabrics available in 100% quilter's cotton.

Adding a border to an existing quilt top should be done with thought and knowledge. The chosen fabric or fabrics should enhance the quilt top. If it can be found, vintage fabric is preferred to reproduction fabric; however, finding a large enough amount to border a quilt can be difficult. Becky Herdle spent three years looking for enough vintage fabric to finish one top before deciding to choose from yardage available today. Because so many reproduction fabrics are almost a perfect simulation of the original fabrics, they are often to be preferred over vintage fabrics that don't quite match.

*1860s Indigo and Pink Fan rest on top of reproduction fabric created by Liz Porter and Marianne Fons with the help of Shirley McElderry's fabric collection.*

As in Option 4, the placement of the fabric border should be measured from the center out so that it is straight. Because quilts were most often quilted from the center out, the outside sections are often quite uneven. On a bed, this doesn't matter, but on a wall, irregularity shows.

Adding a border to a fragment of a quilt will often create a wall hanging which has both depth and balance. You machine sew the border onto the quilt fragment as if it were a pillow. Then lay the quilt fragment with sewn border onto a new backing. Cut batting panels a few inches bigger than the width of the border fabric. Hand or machine baste batting to the quilt edge. Lay border fabric over batting and pin-baste for quilting. Hand quilt in the same way as a larger quilt.

This method is particularly good for badly damaged quilts cut down in size because the quilted framework strengthens the piece.

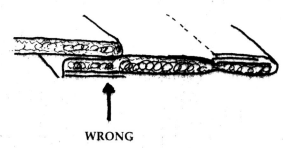

**WRONG**

*Do not overlap batting or fabric when adding border.*

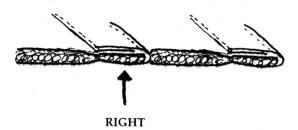

**RIGHT**

*Join all sections so that batting abuts batting.*

# Bindings

Binding a quilt is the finishing step in quiltmaking. The concept is easy: any quilt needs to have its outer edges finished in some manner to prevent the raw edges from fraying and the inner batting from falling out. Although the function of all bindings is the same, the methods used to bind off a quilt are myriad.

# Self-Bound Quilts

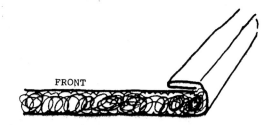

FRONT

## Back-to-Front

A very common method of binding used throughout quilt history was to allow enough extra backing fabric before hand-quilting. After the quilting, the left-over fabric was trimmed to size and rolled or folded to the front. Early chintz cut-out applique quilts were commonly bound off this way. In earlier quilts, the backing was usually trimmed to a scant ⅛" to ¼". The fabric appears almost to have been rolled over rather than folded. The rolled look gives the appearance of a narrow piped edge.

Later quilts show wider fold-overs from the backing—anywhere from ½" to ⅔". On a self-bound quilt, the size of the fold-over does not indicate the date because the sizes varied according to the quiltmaker's wish or whim for that quilt.

If a colorful backing was used, the quiltmaker might decide to make the binding more prominent to enhance the finished look. If the backing were ordinary, the quiltmaker would perhaps choose to minimize the effect. The finished width of the fold-over was also determined by the amount of fabric left after quilting. If a few inches were leftover on all sides, the quiltmaker could be more generous with the binding width.

Machine-stitched self-bound quilts can be dated from 1860 forward. The absence of a machine-stitched quilt binding more likely indicates the lack of a sewing machine than a wish to bind by hand. It is not uncommon to see a machine-stitched finish on a finely appliqued wedding quilt; this would indicate that many quiltmakers did not see the binding as an important aspect of the quilt. At the other extreme, some quiltmakers invested hundreds of hours in fancy borders.

## Front-to-Back

Front-to-back bindings are less common than back-to-front. Common sense prevails again. It is more likely that the quiltmaker chose the best fabric for the top of the quilt and the less important fabric for the backing. A narrow rolled amount of muslin would not violate most finished quilts. However, most quiltmakers would not want to turn over ¼" to ½" of a finished pieced top unless it had been planned prior to assembling the three layers.

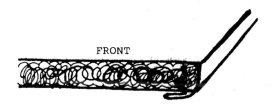

Because there is usually backing left after the quilting process, a self-bound quilt is most likely to be back-to-front. When a quilt design has a large bordering print or solid which seems overwhelming to the framed design, it is more commonly finished off by the front-to-back method.

Late 19th-and early 20th-century quilts were often created to include large borders which are turned under to the back with a generous ½" to 1" fold over. The quilt is hand quilted with the turnover in mind. Once the cable or cross hatch quilting has been finished, the quilt is turned over on a table so that the backing and batting can be carefully trimmed to the appropriate size.

## Invisibly Self-Bound

When the raw edge of both the backing and the top are folded inward, like the fold of pre-made bias binding and sewn together, the edge is self-bound. The front and back folds are slip stitched so closely that the back and front layers are perfectly butted. Many 19th-century quilts are self-bound using a running stitch to hold the top and back together.

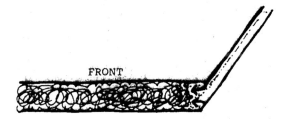

All of the above methods may be used to bind off an old quilt without introducing any other fabric and with minimal loss of fabric from the quilt. Choose whichever method best suits the particular quilt. Trim away all excess fabric and batting and re-sew the raw edges closed.

All three of these finishings are also applicable to the border additions described above or if a border is being trimmed down. When an additional fabric is used to create a border or recover a border, the same methods can be used for finishing the edge. Think of the added fabric as the quilt top edge and either fold it under or over to achieve the desired effect.

## Separate Bindings

Separate bindings have always existed side by side with self-bound quilts. The way of finishing off a quilt indicates the quiltmaker's preference more than any standardized method. There are certain guidelines to follow for historical authenticity, but as in all mediums there are always exceptions that break the rules.

As stated above, many quilts were finished by machine—either on one side or both. As Jonathan Holstein points out, "The presence of a machine-run edge, the long and boring finish of a quilt, as the only element of mechanical work in a great quilt a century or more old, speaks eloquently of the presence of the machine in the next room, or at a neighbor's house. . ."[31]

*Log Cabin c. 1880. When this quilt's binding became frayed a new polyester red and white gingham border was added badly. Note the violation of the Log Cabin design so that logs are covered by the added binding. The binding was removed and replaced by a narrow binding.*

The major decision to make prior to rebinding is whether to remove the old binding before adding the new or whether to sew on the new binding strip and then trim away the old. Both ways are acceptable most of the time. *But*

*beware! There are times when one must remove the old binding prior to rebinding an old quilt. Detailed geometric borders need to be considered before adding a binding. If the binding will cover over part of a crisp right angle, then all the old fabric needs to be removed before the new binding is applied.*

### Straight Bindings

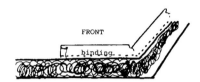

*Machine sew the binding to the front of the quilt.*

*Hand sew the binding to the back.*

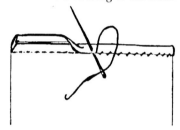

### Scallop Binding

*Scallop edge binding with bias cut stripes.*

*Hand sew binding to back.*

## Types of Binding

**1700—1860**

Narrow binding separate or applied
 ⅛" to ¼"
Twill tape: handwoven or factory loomed
Continuous or 4 separate strips
 straight grain
Straight grain
Scallops, Prairie Points, half-circles
Hand knotted macrame/lace edging

**1870s—1910**

Narrow binding separate or applied
 ¼" to ½"
Twill tape rarely seen
Continuous strip or 4 separate strips

**1880—1900**

Victorian quilts self-bound velvet
 narrow ½" to 15" wide
Mitered corners
4 separate strips common
Hand knotted silk twist/lace
Ruffles from ribbon or folded
Silk/taffeta/moire/satin

**1920—1940**

Pre-made bias bindings
 ½", ⅜",1"
Scallop edges popular
Four separate strips of wider size
Back-to-front common

**Amish**

Traditional 1" binding folded over to
 1" back with four separate
 pieces of fabric

The most effective method of rebinding is to machine sew the binding strip to the front of the quilt, trim away all excess and hand sew the raw edge to the back of the quilt. Even a narrow ⅛" to ¼" can be applied in this way by cantilevering the sewing machine position so that it sews very closely to the edge of the fabric.

Sewing machines were as popular among quilters as rotary cutters are today. Holstein's assessment of the impact of the sewing machine is valid: *"Godey's,* February 1854, in an article entitled, 'The New Sewing Machine,' took its first notice of the invention. . . .By 1855 it was saying: 'These valuable aids to female industry are becoming quite a familiar thing in private families.' In one year in the 1870s, 600,000 sewing machines were sold.

"Machines were extensively employed in piecing quilt tops; about half of all quilts we have seen which date from the 1860s on are machine pieced. Some applique quilts are also machine worked, but they are the exception. The sewing machine was commonly used in both types, even if the quilts were otherwise completely worked by hand, for finishing edges, a boring job." [32]

### Your Own Book of Samples

Making samples is a very effective way to experiment with different sized bindings. Each sample sheet will list the width of the binding, the position of the needle and stitch length, the amount trimmed from the sides and the number of turns on the fabric prior to sewing. These sample sheets save time because the finished product is shown as well as the way to recreate it. For example:

A 1½" strip can be folded over in such a way that the finished binding ranges in size from ⅛" to ¼".

A 1½"-wide strip folded for application = ⅛" finished.

A 1½"-wide strip unfolded for application = ¼" finished.

The width of the binding strip is as important as the foldover of the binding. For this reason it is important to create your own samples because each sewer will handle the binding differently.

Older sewing machines do not cantilever their needles. Several methods can be used to adjust the position. Use the foot as the guide and position the fabric so that it is following a guide within the foot's shape. If preferred, allow more fabric width and know that this will be trimmed away to create a narrow binding.

# Binding Problems

### Exact binding

If the exact binding is necessary to keep the quilt authentic, several solutions are possible. Self-binding can be done on the sides where the binding is badly frayed. It is very common to see older quilts with 2 sides bound and 2 sides self-bound or 3 sides bound and one side self-bound. "Many quiltmakers felt no compulsion to put symmetrical borders on their quilts. The quilt with a border on three sides, two sides or only one side is surprisingly common throughout the history of patchwork quilts." [33]

If the binding is fraying at the folded edge and the exact binding is to be kept, the fraying can be stopped by stabilizing it with a bonded piece of cotton. Remove the binding and iron it flat. Fuse the Wonder Under to a closely coordinating cotton. Cut the bonded fabric into thin

strips ⅛" to ¼" wide and fuse with a hot iron to the fraying center-line of the binding. Avoid bonding sew line of fabric. Re-apply binding to quilt. This method will keep the binding fabric from fraying more.

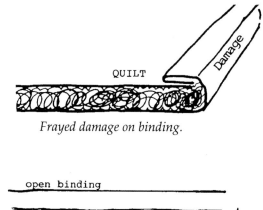

*Frayed damage on binding.*

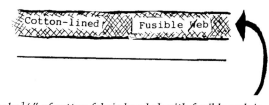

*Apply ¼" of cotton fabric bonded with fusible web in order to stop binding from further fraying.*

### Stealing Binding or Curving a Square

In order to steal binding from a quilt to give it back to the quilt, the shape must be altered slightly. Many quilts have two or four curved corners. By rounding corners of an old quilt, one can usually have enough fabric to repair small rips here and there.

Decide how big the curve edge will be. Salad and cereal bowl are instant circles which will give a wide variation in the size of the curve. On a square edged quilt, the two sides are like two sides of a right triangle and a slight curve is roughly equivalent to one side of the same triangle.

Do not cut the binding ! Hem rip open and safety pin back as much binding as will be necessary for an effective curve. Ease

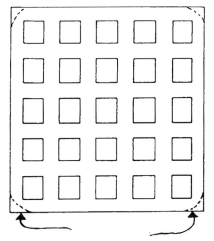

*Curving a square edge in order to eliminate damage or repair rips in binding.*

the binding and pin it into position. When pinned in place, allow for the overlap or turn-under and only then cut off the excess.

## Bedsprings

The old metal bedsprings were notorious for discoloring and ripping old quilts. Often a quilt will be tattered along one side and it is obvious that it was ripped by friction through many years of use. The binding is often intact and can be kept in the same manner by following the procedure described above. The torn section can be cut from the quilt and the original binding can be re-applied.

## Solid Colors

Solid colors are always a good choice to rebind a quilt if no print fabric is found that truly matches the quilt. Hundreds of solids are available in 100% quilter's cotton and if the color is difficult to match, cotton fabric can be dyed to match. (See Resources). The most difficult solids to match are those that have faded for 50 years or more. Many of these solids, typically found in applique quilts, are not truly a color, but rather a blend of colors— reds that have faded to not quite pink or greens that have faded to not quite green or not quite blue.

## Handy Products

Shirley McElderry recommends using Seams Great to cover a ragged binding. This soft sheer strip comes in different colors. It allows the fraying binding to be stabilized without adding to the original quilt, doing for a frayed binding what Crepeline does for fraying fabric.

When in doubt about color, the best choice is natural, cream, bleach or unbleached muslin. Thousands of quilts are simply finished off with a narrow edging of muslin or plain weave cotton.

## Twill Tape/Rug Tape/Ribbons

Woolen quilts from the late 1800s are often finished with a twill tape binding that is attached with a running stitch. Very early quilts may be finished with a narrow hand woven or loomed tape similar to what we would call a twill tape. Victorian quilts are often bound off with satin ribbons and more rarely with velvet ribbons.

## Stitching on Bindings

Stitching should carefully imitate the existing stitches. If tiny overcasting stitches are used on the original, the binding should reflect the original finish. The only exception to this rule of imitation: when completely rebinding a quilt which was machine stitched, hand finishing one side gives the binding a finer look. One trick to finishing off a binding by hand is to line up 12 needles, each threaded and knotted. A piece of foam or a rolled up towel is fine for holding the threaded needles. With threads prepared, it takes about three hours to hand finish a full size quilt on one side.

*Crazy Quilt c. 1900. This kind of narrow binding was often used on Crazy Quilts.*

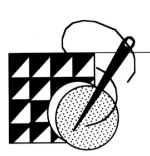

# 6

# Unfinished Quilt Tops
# or Squares

QUILT TOPS, SQUARES OR FRAGMENTS are often inherited or purchased by quilt lovers.  These unfinished projects from the past are still being discovered in attics, trunks and closets.  Although Brackman points out that many quilt tops lose their historical value with later finishing, Jeannie Spears sees finishing antique tops and quilts as completing "the original quilter's vision, bringing it to a creative and useful fulfillment."  Many quilters and collectors, Spears adds, "theorize that finishing is a form of preservation." [34]

Pristine, because they have not been used, they often inspire the owner to do some finishing.  The decision to finish a quilt top or to create a quilt top from squares is an individual choice.  As stated earlier, museum quality quilts, and in this case quilt tops, should not be violated.  If by chance a rare Broderie Perse quilt top is found, it is probably best to do nothing to it.  To finish a pre-Civil War quilt top using later fabrics is to violate a rare historical artifact.  (See p. 14 in Chapter I for photo of Broderie Perse.)

The chances of finding such a rare quilt top today is probably a million to one; however, if the owner does not know the vintage or rarity of the quilt top, it is best to seek some expert advice on the date.

*Album Quilt Top, c. 1850-60. Civil War vintage quilt top has strong historical value. Birds and butterflies appliqued at a later date in contrasting fabric indicate that the quiltmaker's fiance or husband may have died. Butterflies and birds, symbols of immortality, were added to each applique block so that two birds or butterflies are joined forever. Because of the vintage, condition and historical importance of this bridal quilt top transformed into a mourning quilt top, this piece is best left as is.*

## Fringed Seams

Fortunately, most quilt tops and squares are utilitarian and quite sturdy.  If they have stains of any kind, they should never be washed in a machine because the raw edges of the sewn seams will fray into fringe.  Fringed seams which tear apart are very common on quilt tops that have previously been laundered.  To repair weak seams that have very little seam allowance left, one can create thin ⅛" strips of lightweight bonded interfacing or one can create a bonded interfacing to match the color of the quilt top. (See illustration in Chapter V, page 64, for frayed bindings.) Iron the frayed seam flat and apply a thin strip to reinforce the frayed edge. After all the frayed seams have been reinforced in this way, the seams may be resewn.

This same method may be used to reinforce seams that have frayed badly within a quilt. The ⅛" strip of bonded interfacing can be bonded to the underside of the fabric to keep the fabric from further fraying. The bonding gives the fabric enough stability so that the seam does not have to be tugged together which would distort the shape of the quilt design.

## Coverlet Finish

Quilt tops that will be used as summer spreads or table covers may be simply finished by adding a piece of muslin to the back and binding off the edge. This simple method will prevent the seams from being exposed to constant friction. Quilt tops, like quilts, cannot accept repeated friction; it simply wears them out.

Quilt tops and squares may be used in parts in a variety of projects. For centuries, seamstresses created quilted pillows, bags, table covers, clothing, slippers and tea cozies. Leftover scraps from one project always found their way into another, and women's publications in the 19th century were filled with projects for quilted household items as well as bedjackets and decorative details on clothing.

When finishing a quilt top, you may want to add a border to enlarge it; multiple borders may be added to frame and mat the quilt top's color scheme. Busy 1930s quilt tops often look quite stunning when finished with soft baby blue or blue chambray borders. A review of Chapter V on borders and bindings will remind you of various other options.

## Creativity

When a quilt top, squares or fragments are damaged or the remaining sections and pieces are limited, a creative playfulness may come to your rescue. In our everyday life, objects get broken, and this forces us to rethink about how to use them. If our favorite teapot develops a fissure, we may turn it into a planter for a beautiful silk flower arrangement.

Quiltmakers have always brought creativity to their problem solving, and it is the very quilts which show this unique vision that are most remembered. *Old Glories: Magical Makeovers for Vintage Textiles, Trims and Photos* by Diane Herbort and Susan Greenhut as well as *Creating Scrapbook Quilts* by Ami Simms are two excellent books brimming with possibilities. Quilt fragments may frame old family photos, letters and marriage and birth certificates transferred onto cloth. Or, zooming in the opposite direction, quilt fragments and a few shoebox squares may appear within a contemporary wall quilt.

The 1870s quilt shown on p. 69 is sedate in many ways with its four corner Log Cabin blocks and its traditional designs. Yet hidden within a traditional format are two miniature quilts that seem to laugh at convention. Why are they there? Simply because the quiltmaker liked them. "Ha! Ha!" she seems to be saying, "You think this an ordinary quilt, but it has surprises."

The same kind of creative playfulness shows in the Fleur de Lis splendor of peaches and cream in the detail below. Those bouncy yo-yo rosettes are appliqued all over the quilt.

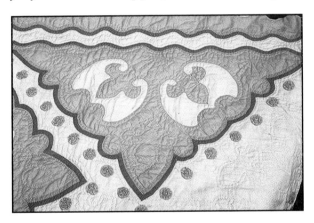

*Exquisitely appliqued and quilted, this joyful 1930s Fleur de Lis Quilt has lots of everthing–quilting, applique, yo-yos and borders. The scalloped edge is invisibly self-turned and edged with a bias applique which mirrors the scalloped edge. This quilt was made by an accomplished needle woman, probably Canadian.*

## Batting or Fillers

King size 100% cotton flannel sheets make wonderful batting for both hand tying and hand quilting. The flannel can simulate the look and feel of older quilts without having to be quilted in every square inch. Prior to using a flannel sheet, wash and dry it for shrinkage before inserting.

All batting manufacturers will send samples of their batting to interested customers. Samples help in deciding on the density or lightness for a particular quilt finish. (See Resources at back of book.)

No one batting is the only perfect batting for each quilter. Undulating quilt tops that poof in waves when laid across a bed or table usually require high loft battings to minimize the poor piecing. Using a low loft batting on erratically pieced quilt tops only emphasizes the original quiltmaker's mistakes. Finely finished quilt tops take well to low loft battings, flannel and cotton. The quilt finisher must decide which batting will best suit the quilt top.

Cotton battings have come a long way with new light glazing that helps hold the cotton fibers together and allows quilters to create more open designs. New products continue to be developed for the quilt market, such as Warm & Natural. It is made of cotton needlepunched onto a scrim that keeps the cotton fibers from migrating and gives the look and feel of the older quilt batting. The older kind of cotton batting must be quilted every square inch so that a pocket can be formed to contain the batting. If it's not contained, the batting will lump and fall to one end of the quilt.

## Ties vs. Quilting

Quilting takes time, and many unfinished quilt tops exist today simply because the makers never had the time or money to finish them. Hand quilting a full size quilt top takes 50 to 500 to 1,000 hours depending on the complexity of the design. Such a commitment of time explains why there are so many unquilted tops.

One way to handle the time commitment is to break the quilting time into smaller segments by first tying the quilt. This method allows the quilter to have a finished quilt top which then can be quilted hoop by hoop as time allows.

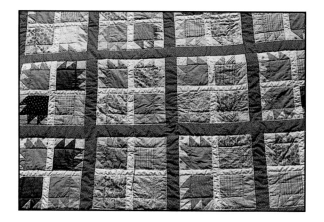

*Bear Paw Quilt c. 1890, hand quilted 1992. This top (shown in detail) could have been tied first and then quilted one square at a time as time allowed .*

Ties may be used as a permanent finish as well as a temporary finish. Back, batting and top are layered as for hand quilting. The three layers are pinned together to keep them from moving. Once all the squares are pinned, a long embroidery needle with crochet thread or DMC floss is used to secure the three layers together.

*Tied comforters typically have overhand knot to the front.*

*Crazy Quilts and Log Cabin Quilts have overhand knot to back.*

Whether the ties are in the back, as on Crazy Quilts and Foundation Log Cabins, or toward the front, as in the tied comforters of the early 1900s, the method used is the same. Ties may either be hidden in the seams of the design or serve to decorate the front of the quilt.

*Two quilt tops from the late 1800s were hand tied in the 1930s, a typical speedy quilt finishing method of the time. The muticolored quilt accepts the multiple ties more easily then the red and white quilt because the red and white quilt's graphic impact is diluted by the red ties.*

Quilts with strong graphic impact such as Log Cabins or Flying Geese keep their dramatic flair by tying them to the back. Busy Scrap Quilts with hundreds of colors can actually be enhanced by having ties come to the front because the ties serve as a focal point of interest amid all the busyness of the prints. Ties may always be removed at a later time, so if you decide you don't like one effect, redo the tying to suit your needs.

Once tied and bound, the quilt may be used as is and hand quilted over time. Hand quilting is most visible on solid colors, and is more visible on light colors than on dark colors. If a minimal amount of quilting is to be done, choose a design that will maximize the impact of the quilting.

*Red and White Irish Chain c. 1880, hand quilted 1980. Quilt owner chose hearts for the quilting design to symbolize her love for her grandmother who, she felt, would have appreciated the completion of the unfinished project.*

## Brittle Fabric

Beware of brittle fabrics which may puncture and break when hand quilted. Often the fabric appears to be sturdy to the touch, but when the quilting process is applied, the needle perforates the fabric as if it were a dotted line on notebook paper. Avoid this fabric wherever it occurs in the quilt even if it means some variation in the quilting design.

Older squares and tops from the 1860s—1880s often contain browns and blacks that seem fine but are rotten because the dyes have tendered the fabric to such a point that they are merely waiting to dissolve into fragments.

Carefully examine each piece of fabric prior to deciding to hand quilt an old top. Be aware that some restoration of these sections may be needed at a later time.

## Finishing Yo-Yos a.k.a. Popcorn & Marguerites

Yo-yo quilts are both wonderful and terrible! Like crocheted bedspreads or fishnetting, they can hook and snag on any and all objects. These funny circles that were made from home and store-bought scraps were first seen as decorative additions to clothing and Victorian Crazy Quilts. In the early twenties, row upon row of yo-yos were whipstitched together to form summer bed covers with great decorative impact.

Yo-yos change their look with the color placed under them and this made them versatile summer spreads. Finishing a yo-yo requires the same process as hand tying a quilt. Unlike a quilt, the fabric chosen for the underlayer of the yo-yo is most important.

*Yo-Yo, 1930. Finished as a summer spread, this yo-yo had green fabric attached to the back. Note how the yo-yos pop out in bas-relief like rosettes on the side of a building.*

If a speckled navy blue is placed beneath the yo-yo, the circles seem to shimmer like colors in an impressionistic painting; if a solid color is placed beneath them, the circles pop out in bas-relief like circular encrustations or rosettes. Choosing the background fabric for the yo-yo is the most important decision to make. The answer will come from placing the yo-yo on different fabrics which often means taking the yo-yo to the fabric store.

Busy prints force the yo-yos to blend into a pointillistic image. Solid black satin behind solid color silk/satin yo-yos can create a stained-glass window effect.

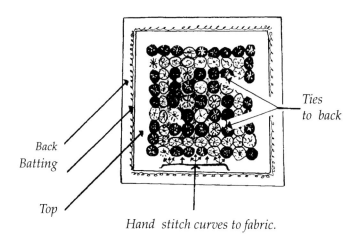

*Ties to back*

*Back*
*Batting*

*Top*

*Hand stitch curves to fabric.*

FINISHING A YO-YO FOR VERTICAL DISPLAY

To make the hanging shown at left, lay the yo-yo top over the fabric. Pin the layers together by forming a grid line that will be followed throughout. It can be easier to measure the entire yo-yo and divide by 5" or 6" to see if it will come out evenly. The ties will be lost in the background. The most important factor is to secure the yo-yos in a consistent pattern, so they will not buckle. Slip stitch the curved edge of the yo-yo to the background fabric and measure out 1" to 2" which will remain as a border or mat for the busy circlets.

A second method is to machine stitch a wide border panel directly onto the yo-yo edge as if you were adding a row of fabric to a quilt top edge. Once turned, the fabric will border the yo-yo and keep it anchored securely in place. If this method is used, a thin layer of batting may be added to the outer border to keep it soft looking. This slightly padded border softens and enhances the textured look of the finished piece.

Both finishes are effective when one wishes to use the yo-yo as a wall piece or a more sturdy bed coverlet. By controlling the underfabric color which integrates the surface complexity, yo-yos can be stunning.

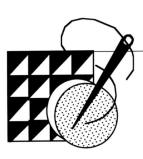

# Victorian Quilts

VICTORIAN CRAZY QUILTS and all other pieced quilts made of silk during the Victorian era are in a special category and cannot be approached in a traditional manner. Victorian Crazy Quilts were created as show quilts and as artistic examples of quiltmakers' needlework skills. They must be handled with the same care that would be given to any pieces of art.

Silk was often dipped in liquid tin both to increase its weight and to add a rustling glaze finish. Five pounds of silk will absorb 10 pounds of liquid tin and, at a time when silk was sold by the pound, it became a practical way to triple the volume of silk. The rustling of silk petticoats and dresses, a sign of elegance, was pleasing to both wearers and beholders, to say nothing of marketers. Remember, even Scarlett O'Hara's mammy asked Rhett Butler to get her a rustling petticoat.

Unfortunately, the fancy piecework and Crazy Quilts so praised by women's publications then are now in fragile and disintegrating condition. Butterfly wings best describe their fragility because the slightest tugging or handling causes fracturing of the silk. "It is unfortunate, "as Judy Wentworth writes," that the manufacturer's practice of weighting silk, by the addition of various substances to make it stiffer and heavier, has caused 19th-century silks to rot, and crumble, in a way that the unleaded silks of the 18th century have not

done. This phenomenon may be seen in all too many of the spectacular Victorian silk patchworks....there is no remedy for once they have become brittle the silks cannot take the pressure of needle or thread." [35]

According to Putnam and Finch, "From about 1870, weighting began to be done excessively. Although some companies did little or no weighting, one firm stated in 1909 that colored silks could be weighted to between fifty and one hundred percent and black silk up to four to five hundred percent. For heavy weighting, the silk could be kept for days in a bath with tin or iron salts." [36]

Quilt restorers have strong opinions on whether Victorian silk quilts can be repaired. I maintain that these splendid jewel-like quilts can be repaired, but they must be repaired differently. It is true that while repairing one damaged section, a needle and thread will puncture the already fragile fabrics and cause double damage.

There are three practical solutions for avoiding double damage. They are netting, fusing and separate reconstructions that can be applied to the quilt. For the purpose of simplicity, I will use the word silk throughout my directions, although taffeta, faille, brocade, satin, tapestry, velvet and corduroy were all used on Victorian Crazy Quilts.

# Netting

Fine Crepeline, tulle or netting can be applied to the damaged sections of a Crazy Quilt. Different shades of netting can be used in order to enhance the fabric underneath. Light beige and white work best for light colors, and taupe or dove grey are best for dark colors.

The netting should be trimmed to the size of the embroidered area so that the light tacking is made on the embroidery threads and not on the silk itself. Geometric designs with no embroidered stitches should be lightly tacked with as few stitches as possible. Match the color thread to the netting color.

Netting with Crepeline contains the flaking silk within the confines of the affixed netting. However, this technique does not keep the silk from continuing to flake and crack. Having seen the results of falling silk over the last ten years, I have concluded that the netting technique is not a stabilizing technique. It is rather a containment technique and will contain only if the textile remains flat in storage. When netted silk is displayed on a wall the silk will fall into the net and create pouch-like protrusions. Because owners begged us to create a more aesthetically pleasing solution, other methods were devised which stabilize the flaking from falling out completely.

# Fusing

Because Victorian Crazy Quilts are most often used as art pieces, they lend themselves to several fusing and bonding techniques. Many smaller crazy quilts are framed so as not to be handled by the viewer. Fused repairs should be seen as aesthetic or cosmetic, so that the wall art will be enjoyed without major sections

fraying and shredding within the frame.

Spread the quilt out on a large table and move it as little as possible. Use a small portable ironing board or ironing table which can be moved from section to section as needed. The next step depends on whether you choose option 1, 2, 3 or 4.

## Option 1

Simple and direct, this method is similar to replacing a broken tile on a floor. A closely matching color of silk, taffeta or brocade is selected and then a piece of fusing web is bonded to the wrong side of the fabric. The chosen fabric now resembles a store bought knee patch and is ready for fusing.

Next, take clear plastic or tracing paper. Place it over the section to be covered and trace its outline with a fine tipped permanent Sharpie pen. Make sure the outline shape remains within the embroidered stitches which will remain showing.

Using the pattern outline, cut out the shape from the bonded fabric. Place the bonded fabric precisely over the section to be covered. Pin a few corners with quilting pins. Anchor the long quilting pin into the ironing board cover the way you would wedge a long quilting pin into a corkboard. This keeps the pin as unobtrusive as possible. Cover the area with a cotton press cloth (or an old sheet) and iron the bonded fabric in place.

## Option 2

When large sections of silk are cracking but have not yet fallen out, the Victorian quilt can be worked on from the back. Crazy Quilts were sewn onto a background fabric and were usually tacked. If there is enough good silk which is ready to dissolve, but which could be stabilized from the back, the following method is recommended.

With a hem ripper, take out all the ties which secure the three layers. Open a large section along one side and very carefully turn the quilt inside out.

A small tool with crocodile action called an ear polypus, a surgical instrument designed to pass through a ⅛" hole and still open and close its jaws, is most helpful in getting at hard to reach spots.

Most unfinished Crazy Quilt backings resemble a cobblestone or flagstone walk. Pin to indicate which sections in the front need stabilizing. With a Wonder Marker make an "X" on the sections that are to be stabilized. Place your ironing table under the chosen section. Think of an envelope which has two sides. The silk is the side that does not open and the backing is the side that will open.

Cut through the cotton backing only so that the cotton can be peeled away from the silk and pinned into the ironing board which has been placed under the section.

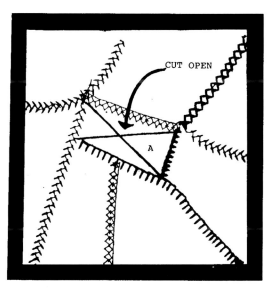

BACK OF VICTORIAN QUILT
*Section to be cut from the back. Fuse web is inserted and envelope-like sections will close on top of fuse web for bonding. See black and white photos below for entire process.*

Cut a piece of Wonder Under to the desired shape of the section to be fused. Place the fusing web on the silk.

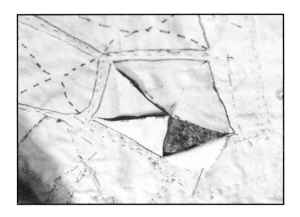

Unpin the cotton flaps of the envelope and carefully reposition the cotton backing fabric into place.

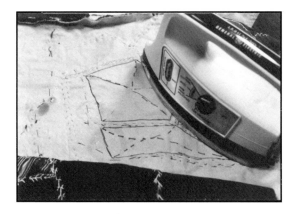

Iron the section with a medium hot, dry iron so that the silk becomes bonded to the cotton backing.

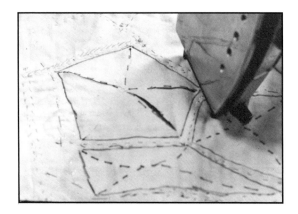

This method is excellent for stabilizing cracking silk in unfinished quilt squares and panels.

## Option 3

When the fragile fabric is cracking in a few sections and there is enough of an opening to stabilize the silk from the top, small pieces of fusing web can be placed with long tweezers or medical scissors with an alligator-like clamping action and positioned under the soon-to-be-flaking silk. Use a press cloth as described in Option 1.

## Option 4

Often beautiful embroidery is the only intact section on a piece of fraying or flaking silk. Netting camouflages and obscures the embroidery. To keep the embroidery intact and in place, a liquid fusing agent can be used. (See Resources.)

*Embroidered Crazy Quilt Panel rests on self-destructing silk. Because remaining cotton threads will continue to give the embroidery stability, fine netting may be gently applied to the embroidered stitches along the edge.*

This is an overnight project. Lay the quilt out flat so that each section can remain flat for six to eight hours. Generously squeeze out liquid fuse so that it coats evenly. Clear Fray Check is the easiest to use and dries clearly, leaving a stabilized embroidery that would otherwise fall out or be partially obscured with netting.

## Painted Flowers and Figures

*Kate Greenaway figures resting on self-destructing silk may fall out with time. Netting over the lavender square will help to keep the figures where they belong, however. If the silk dissolves into powdery ash, fragile embroidery will fall with them.*

Often the painted decorations on Victorian Crazy Quilts crack into small shards; netting will not stop these cracked fractures from falling out. But liquid fusing agents are able to glue the pieces together in the same way that one would glue the broken pieces of a beautiful piece of porcelain. Although the piece of porcelain is cracked and glued, its beauty will remain to give us pleasure.

So-Sheer Fusible Knit is recommended by Kaethe Kliot, the lace expert at LACIS (see Resources), to stabilize fragile silks. Kliot says the silk remains soft but is protected against further flaking.

## Separate Reconstructions

Victorian Crazy Quilts with overall embroidered seams may be sewn. However they should not be sewn in a conventional manner because conventional "patching" techniques, as already noted, cause destruction of other sections while one section is being repaired.

Think of the embroidery floss as the strongest links to stability. By reproducing an embroidered "patch" or tile in the desired color and size, the embroidery floss can be joined together so that floss becomes a kind of grouting that keeps the tiles in place.

*INTERLACING EMBROIDERY TO EMBROIDERY*

*Imagine that the letters are embroidery stitches. By creating a reconstructed section with embroidered edges, the embroidery of patch A can be interlaced with the embroidery of the existing quilt and the fragile Victorian fabric will be moved and handled very few times. No sewing into the quilt takes place.*

The following illustrations detail the interlacing of embroidered stitches.

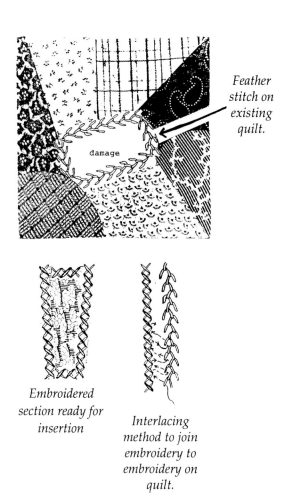

*Feather stitch on existing quilt.*

damage

*Embroidered section ready for insertion*

*Interlacing method to join embroidery to embroidery on quilt.*

Review Option 1 under Fusing. The same method is used to make an exact tracing of the section to be replaced. (See also Self-Turned Applique method in Chapter III.)

Thick brocade or velvet can be prepared as in Option 1 but this fabric creates a great deal of bulk when turned under. I recommend cutting the thick fabric to exact size and applying a thin coat of liquid clear Fray Check to the outside edge. Let this dry overnight on a flat surface. Many Victorian Crazy Quilts had velvet appliques which were not turned under.

## Embroidery

Embroidery of the finished patch can be done by hand or by machine. Traditional embroidery stitches are illustrated in many books and need not be complex to be effective. The three most commonly used stitches are the feather, the cross stitch and the buttonhole.

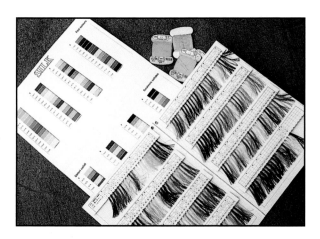

Wonderful silk threads are available in a wide array of colors, and perle cotton can at times be closer to the texture of the embroidery floss on the antique quilt. (See Resources.)

### Silks

If the created patch is applied by hand, use an embroidery needle threaded with a complementary floss which will suit your particular crazy quilt.Pin the center of the patch so that it is properly positioned and begin using any desired embroidery stitch so that the embroidery floss remains on the patch and weaves in and out of the adjoining embroidery. This method resembles joining two crochet sections or two knitted sections. All stress is placed on the created patch and on the embroidery floss.

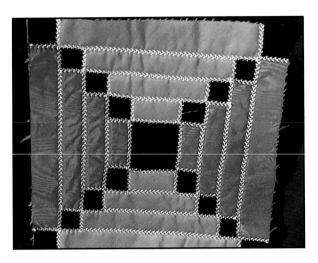

*Machine Feather Stitching. Using DMC cotton perle #8 and a size 19 or 20 needle closely imitates hand embroidery.*

## Machine Embroidery

Sewing machines can reproduce hand embroidery so that a trained eye cannot detect the difference. Stitch and Tear is a must for this method because it gives the created patch the necessary stability for receiving the embroidery.

Place the patch onto an oversized piece of Stitch and Tear. (See Resources.) Select a decorative stitch that is simple and geometric such as the overcast, buttonhole, or feather stitch. Even the zigzag stitch can be effectively used. Use a high gloss thread which complements the overall quilt. Instead of using one strand of this thread, use two to three strands, whichever the bobbin accepts. If you have only one spool of thread to use, make several bobbins of this color and mount all the bobbins on your sewing machine spool holder. Then run two or three threads from all the bobbins at once.

On a practice piece of fabric, adjust the stitch length and width for the desired effect which will decorate the outside edge of the patch. The machine embroidery should puncture the outer edge of the patch so that the embroidery abuts the existing embroidery.

Wonderful machine embroidery can be achieved using DMC cotton perle #8 and a size 19 or 20 needle. The same method is used as described above, except for the needle size and thread size. Due to the thickness of the floss, wider and longer stitches are recommended.

## Sample Sheets

Creating a sample sheet of decorative stitches can save hours of work. Simply play with different threads and settings on your own sewing machine. As stitch widths and lengths are changed, write the adjustment change on your sample sheet. These sample stitches will allow you to adjust your machine at a later date to reproduce the desired effect.

If your sewing machine does the zigzag stitch only, you can outline the patch with a long and wide zigzag stitch and then add French knots or a few Lazy Daisy petals to the stitching.

Before attaching the embroidered patch to the Crazy Quilt, remove all pieces of Stitch and Tear. The Stitch and Tear embeds itself into the embroidered edge of the patch. Wide edged tweezers are excellent for pulling away all the perforated pieces of the backing.

## Lace and Ribbons

Many Victorian Crazy Quilts were decorated with lace or ribbons. Similar to netting application, fine old lace or even exquisite new lace can be carefully applied using the exact method described for adding netting. Black, brown, ecru and white laces are the most common colors found on original Crazy Quilts. (See Resources.)

Ribbons were lavishly integrated into many old Crazy Quilts and often the ribbons were aligned side by side. This method can be effectively used because ribbons have pre-finished edges and create little bulk. Many contemporary ribbons in fine sewing stores offer reproductions of 19th-century designs. Silk ribbons are still being produced in England by the original method used in the Victorian era.

## Do Nothing

Although doing nothing sounds absurd, it can be a very effective technique provided the backing of the Victorian square is compatible with the overall Crazy Quilt.

Quite often, a quiltmaker would use glazed cotton for the quilt foundation. If the floral or colored foundation fabric under the flaking silk blends with the totality, one can remove all flaking and fraying silk with tweezers and fine-tipped scissors. Once the telltale signs of shredded fabric are removed, the remaining embroidery stitches create the illusion that the backing piece is the intended segment of the Crazy Quilt.

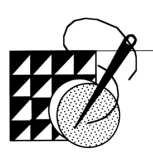

# 8

# *Sewing Techniques Review*

*Wednesday, mending.*

FIFTY YEARS AGO, this chapter would not have been included in this book. At that time, most women already had the basic sewing skills as part of their repertoire. A hundred and fifty years ago, the topic would not even have been discussed by adult women because it was assumed that all women had this knowledge at their fingertips. Cookbooks do not describe how to shop for the ingredients. Likewise, the Godey's and Peterson books for women of the 1800s did not give directions for making their designs because the editors assumed that their readers could replicate them.

## *Traditional Sewing Knowledge and Skills*

Monday, Washing; Tuesday, Ironing; Wednesday, Mending. This triad of domestic obligations has been immortalized in many embroidered panels from the turn of the century. Lucy Larcom in her 1889 *New England Girlhood* emphasizes the importance of both making and mending clothes. [37] Mending all clothing and household linens extended their use. Indeed, this task was so important that one day of the week was set aside for sewing and mending of all kinds.

Quilt restoration depends on all of the traditional skills used in ordinary mending and fine mending. Some women actually specialized in fine invisible mending and were sought out for their expert ability to repair holes and tears in clothing and fine textiles. But all women were expected to make and mend clothing and household linens. Because quilts were part of their sewing repertoire, quilts were continually being mended as well as patched.

Sewing skills require the repetition of simple techniques. The *Good Housekeeping Needlecraft Encyclopedia* states: "Needlework is a game with very simple rules, rules that may or may not be followed by the player when designing. . . .The designing of needlework apparently defies all rules, and yet is an application of the basic rules. The finished piece of needlework is always a presentation of the needlewoman's understanding of her subject, of her love and admiration of the hand arts." [38] This quote is just as valid if we substitute the word "quilting" for needlework, or if we substitute the words "quilt restoration" for needlework.

Before starting work on restoring a beloved quilt, it is useful to make your own workbook of traditional stitches. I recommend practicing each of the following stitches and then stapling a sample of each to a looseleaf paper for keeping in a three-ring binder. By practicing the stitches without the stress of achieving perfect sewing, you will develop your own rhythm. The notebook may contain not only samples, but reminders for certain handling that is effective, such as, "This stitch works best left to right for me," or "Use size 10 needle to get this look." Whatever can be written, will help you to achieve the same effect again without having to re-practice.

*Sample sheets which can be made to use for later reference. The more personal and precise, the easier it is to use.*

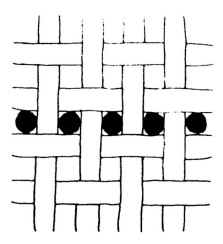

*Fine mending requires that the needle and single thread punctures and picks up ONE thread at a time.*

In all hand sewing, the size of the stitch is controlled by the number of threads picked up by the needle. Fine sewing refers to techniques which require picking up a single thread with the needle. Fine sewing is best achieved with fine needles, but can be achieved with larger needles in the hand of an accomplished seamstress. Ordinary sewing refers to techniques which require larger spacing and picking up three to ten threads per needle.

## Straight of Grain vs. Bias

Take a piece of used cotton sheeting and cut out a 12" square piece of fabric. Using the illustrations below, cut out a 2" wide piece along the grain of the fabric——right to left, or top to bottom. Next, cut a piece from the remaining 8" square along the diagonal.

Tug at the piece cut on the straight of grain and next tug at the piece cut on the bias. No words can describe the surprise of actually feeling the bias cut stretch in one's hands. Any fabric cut on the bias requires different handling from fabric cut on the grain. Straight of grain and bias will be referred to throughout the text. Although these terms are used repeat-

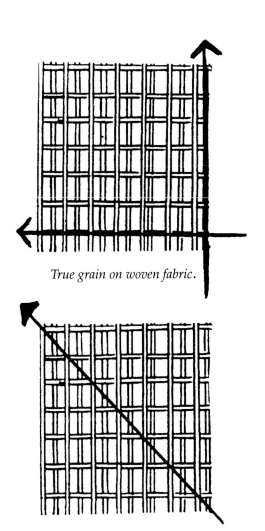

*True grain on woven fabric.*

*True bias on woven fabric.*

## Running Stitch

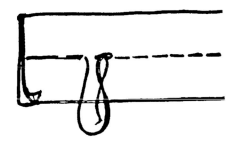

The running stitch is made by passing the needle in and out of the material in a horizontal line. Several stitches are usually put on the needle before it is pulled through. It is the most universal stitch used in all sewing categories, in all cultures.

❦ Two pieces of fabric are sewn together by hand using this stitch.

❦ Hand application of binding uses the running stitch on one side and the blind stitch on the other.

❦ Twill tape application uses the running stitch.

❦ Self-bound quilts often use the running stitch.

❦ Sunbonnet Sue appliques from the 1930s have black embroidery made with the running stitch.

edly in quilting manuals and sewing books, their importance can not be stressed enough.

Quilt restoration must include concern for the thread direction on fabric because thread direction must be considered when mending or darning. The grain of the added fabric must match the grain of the receiving fabric. Natural light falls differently on fabric cut on the straight of grain than it does on fabric cut on the bias. If one applies a bias cut fabric onto a straight of grain, on any solid color, the repaired section will be twice as noticeable. A magnifying glass is helpful in seeing the thread directions on fabric.

❦ Signatures on quilts at times were sewn with this stitch.

❦ Quilting is a running stitch applied to layers of fabric and an inner liner. All of hand quilting is really a variation of the running stitch.

## Backstitch

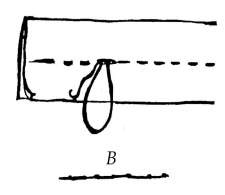

*B*

BACKSTITCH

*The backside of the running stitch looks the same as the top side. The backside of the backstitch resembles B in the illustration and looks like one continuous overlapping thread as if it were the outline stitch illustrated on the Popular Embroidery Stitches Chart at the end of the chapter.*

Backstitch is the running stitch with a second stitch going back over half the length of the previous running stitch. Backstitching has often been used by quiltmakers, and it is for this reason that some quilt pieces sewn by hand are so difficult to hemrip. One is actually ripping out two stitches interlocked with each other. It is the strongest kind of handstitching for hand-piecing.

## Even Basting Stitch

Even basting stitch is a running stitch which is ½" long. It can be used to hold hand applique in place to secure three layers of quilt before quilting, and to tack down the outer edge of a velvet Victorian border to keep it from loosening from the back.

## Hemming Stitch

Hemming stitch can be any tiny overhand stitch which uses a small slanting stitch and takes up a few threads in the cloth and on the fold. Bindings from 1870 to the present are often sewn with this stitch.

HEMMING STITCH

## Vertical Hemming

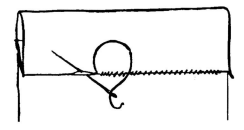

VERTICAL HEMMING STITCH

Vertical hemming stitch is the same as above except that the stitch is taken perpendicularly. This vertical hemming stitch is common on many pre-Civil War applique quilts and on Broderie Perse quilts. The tiny vertical hemming stitches are often as close as 15 to 20 stitches per inch.

## Blind Hemming Stitch

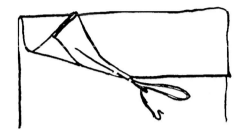

BLIND HEMMING STITCH

Blind hemming stitch is the same as above except that tiny stitches are placed on fold so as to be barely visible on the right side of the work. This stitch is effective for applique in quilt restoration.

## Ladder Stitch

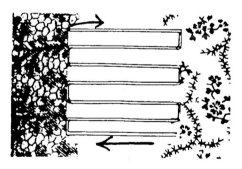

LADDER STITCH

Ladder stitch, recommended by the quilt restorer, Shirley McElderry, who shared her restoration technique in *American Quilter*, is the core of Ami Simms' book, *Invisible Applique*. [39] This simple stitch is a true blind stitch which

can be mastered within a short practice session and is invaluable for restoration of pieced and applique quilts.

Take one stitch in the fold of the patch being applied. Then begin a stitch in the existing patch directly opposite where the first stitch ended; then go back and make another stitch in the patch being applied; repeat. After two or three stitches, snug the two patches together and continue. This makes an invisible seam and is very kind to fragile fabrics because the tension can be exactly adjusted.

## Whipstitch

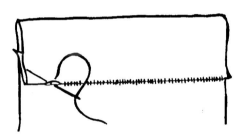

WHIPSTITCH

Whipstitch or overcast stitch refers to a simple hemming stitch which is noticeably visible. This stitch is often seen on bindings and appliques. Early whipstitched appliques may have 10 to 15 stitches per inch. English paper piecing methods usually show whipstitching.

## French Seam

French seam is often seen on summer spreads and coverlets with applique squares. Because the outer edge of the quilt square is the only raw edge, the squares are sewn with the two wrong sides together. This seam is trimmed closely and the squares are then sewn with the

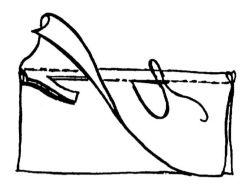

*FRENCH SEAM*

two right sides together. This leaves the first seam sewn within the second seam, and the summer spread will not unravel. A type of French Seam is seen on the back of 1930 quilts which used "apartment quilting", techniques popularized by the McKim studio. "Apartment quilting" is a version of quilt-as-you-go.

Darning is an excellent technique for repairing moth holes as well as holes in Marseille spreads and overshot blankets. The threads or yarn should closely match the existing color. Darning recreates the missing bridge work by reweaving the pattern over created bridge work. Although many of us have the memory of mothers and grandmothers who darned stockings, this technique was also used on cloth by placing a piece of closely matching fabric under the fragile section.

Remember those potholders which were made years ago on metal frames? Darning works in much the same way. Vertical lines are created with thread and horizontal lines of thread are woven in and out of the vertical lines so that the finished work resembles a fine mesh screen.

## Darning

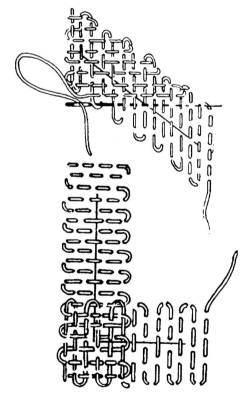

*DARNING*

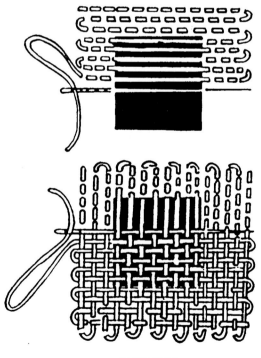

*DARNING*

An inverted bowl serves the same function as a darning egg. Place the hole over the bottom of the bowl in order to give the needle a hard surface to work on. Begin to build thin layers of thread in a matching color so that you create linear threads on a screen. Then weave in the opposite direction. An effective darned section remains evenly filled and flat.

## Darning Dangers:

❧ Pulling threads too tightly which creates puckers.

❧ Using too many threads that add bulk.

❧ Picking up too many threads so that the finish is coarse.

Darning well so that the hole disappears in the process, requires great patience and diligence in stitching. Darning cannot be done quickly and for this reason, it is best to do small amounts at one sitting.

## Mending

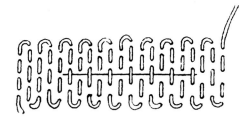

*MENDING*

Like darning, mending is best seen on repair of clothing from the late 1800s. A piece of fabric that matches the color of the clothing to be repaired is placed under the torn or worn section. The piece of added fabric is placed there in order to reinforce the top fabric. Many of the illustrations in *The Care and Preservation of Textiles* refer to a couching stitch that is a darning stitch taken at wider intervals. The darning stitch is an in-and-out reweaving at close intervals............ A couching stitch is made at wider intervals.___.___.____.

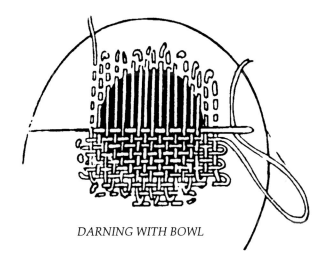

*DARNING WITH BOWL*

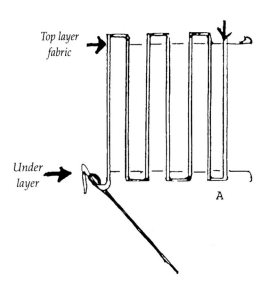

Top layer fabric

Under layer

A

Tiny stitches pierce the top visible layer of fabric while affixing it to the reinforcing fabric underneath. By using tiny stitches that pick up one or two threads on the top layer, this repair can be almost invisible to the eye without magnifying glasses. I once admired a white border fabric which had been meticulously repaired in the late 1800s. The trick to expert work is to keep the thread inconspicuous by making tiny stitches and by running rows of parallel tiny stitches that mirror the grain line in the worn fabric.

The Needlecraft Encyclopedia refers to darning as weaving on a small scale. It is essentially a practical application of the running stitch. Always darn on the right side of the fabric and never make a knot so that there is no strain on the fabric. Be sure to start and end the running stitches far enough beyond the hole so that the mend will not pull out. Never draw the thread tight.[40] Straight tears, three-cornered tears and diagonal tears are all problems that can be solved by mending them with the darning stitch.

## Tiny Darts

When fabric is split in a quilt top, a tiny dart resembling a rolled edge on a handkerchief may be created so that the split fabric is rejoined without having to replace the entire piece of fabric. A close and tiny whipstitch is used to join the split fabric.

## Interlacing

Another way to repair a split on a quilt is with an interlacing stitch. Think of lacing a boot or shoe. The shoe laces are woven in and out of small holes and tightened to bring the two sides of the shoe together. The interlacing stitch

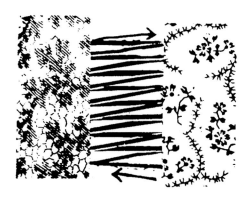

INTERLACING

works much the same way, except the needle and thread do not overlap the fabric. Instead, the thread weaves its way back and forth under the fabric pulling it gently together. This stitch resembles the ladder stitch described above except that the threaded needle works the underside of the torn fabric and exits and re-enters the cloth from side to side. With gentle pulling the two sides of the torn fabric may be joined. The raw edges of the fabric are needle turned to the inside before fabric is pulled together.

## Split Seams

Blindstitch is used so that the thread weaves in and out of the folds of the split seam and gently abuts the split seam. When blindstitching a split seam, the biggest danger is pulling the thread too tightly. The thread should ease the fabric together rather than pucker it.

## Hiding Knots or Locking Threads for Mending

Just as a quilter pops her knots into the middle layer of batting, so can an overhand knot be popped gently between the quilt layers to be repaired. By popping one's knot about a half an inch away from the seam one is approaching, one does not have a knot to handle at the split seam.

Another effective method is to enter the fabric with the threaded needle and leave a long tail in the middle layer. Re-enter the fabric one or two threads over and move the needle back a half inch. Exit and enter the fabric again by picking up one or two threads. The thread is now secure. This method is used to end the sewing process.

## Patching a Hole

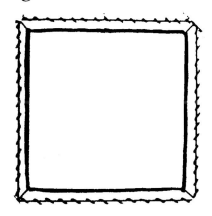

*This is what the inside of a restored square would look like.*

"When the hole is large, it is best to patch. Always cut the hole into a square or rectangle, following the grain of the fabric. Cut a patch ½" to 1½" larger on all sides than the hole. New washable materials should be washed to prevent shrinking after they are made up. In print fabrics, be sure to match the figures and stripes accurately." [41]

### Hemmed Patch

Insert a piece of matching fabric so as to align its grain and design to blend perfectly with the adjoining fabric. From the right side, hem the turned-under edges of the hole to the patch. Use small blind stitches and press. If re-quilting is necessary, re-quilt as needed using the false re-quilting described below. A tailor's ham is very effective in controlling the area to be patched. As the raw edge of the hole is turned under, pin the aligned fabric into the ham. Remove pins as the stitching is made. Pinning the patch into a ham eliminates all the sharp edges of the needle and stabilizes the edges for sewing.

## Embroidery

"Embroidery and music need no interpreters. Embroidery is an international language for all lovers of beauty. . . Analysis of these advanced stitches in embroidery impresses us with the truth that beauty is basically simple. . . the steps are repeated over and over again until their fineness and symmetry make one forget that the finished piece is a mere application of the satin, the buttonhole, the cross, the hemstitch or the darning stitch. . ." [42]

## Embroidery Stitch

*Overall Sam is outlined with the buttonhole stitch in a slightly contrasting color.*

*BLANKET STITCH*      *BUTTONHOLE STITCH*

*EMBROIDERY STITCHES ARE A VARIATION OF
BUTTONHOLE STITCH*

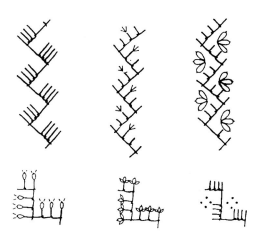

involve the outline stitch, the running stitch and the buttonhole stitch which is also called the blanket stitch. So many books exist on embroidery and are easily accessible, that anyone wishing more detail can find it easily.

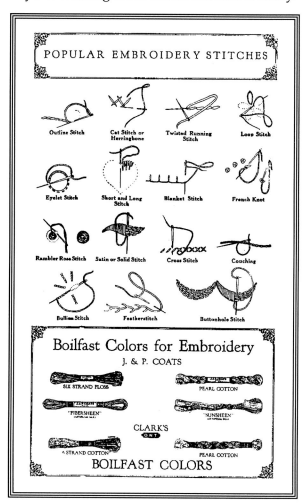

Often, the most magnificent Crazy Quilts have the simple embroidery stitches above in different colored floss. The simple repetition of these basic stitches in different colors creates a mosaic of embroidered complexity. Color variation and repetition are the key to embroidery on Crazy Quilts.

The drawings here show complexity created from simplicity. Sunbonnet Sues, butterflies, and outline embroidery usually

*The Coats and Clark envelope arrived with the needed embroidery patterns, thread and a listing of basic stitches which were to be used in executing the designs.*

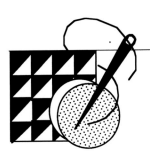

# 9

# TLC for Old Quilts
# (Tender Loving Care)

IF TEN COLLECTORS WERE ASKED how to clean quilts, ten different answers could be expected. Not only would the collectors not agree, each would vehemently argue that his or her way is the best. I have learned to give options and not debate. The ultimate decision to wash or not to wash a quilt and how to wash is up to the individual owner. The options given below are just that–options. The methods described vary because different methods work equally well.

The most dangerous aspect of cleaning any quilt is what it may do to dye rot. Some quilt fabrics were produced by using iron as a mordant to set the dye colors. Unbeknownst to the manufacturers, the iron ate away the cotton fibers in the cloth. Colors notorious for rotting are black, black coffee, deep browns (due to the iron used as mordants) and Turkey red due to the abrasive method used in producing the color.

Any laundering of the aforementioned fabrics will cause them to disappear. The rot cannot be stopped and must simply be accepted. For some reason, the dry cleaning process does not destroy this kind of dye-rot the way laundering does. Hundreds of quilts in this color spectrum have been successfully dry cleaned by my local cleaner. Because I wanted to match the exact results, I have deliberately had one piece of a damaged quilt laundered in water and another piece dry cleaned. Even though I laundered the smaller piece by hand and followed all the rules, much fabric was lost through laundering; almost none, on the other hand, was lost through dry cleaning. Many quilt experts insist that quilts be laundered only. However, in my experience, dye rot is made worse by laundering.

Not cleaning a quilt is the least stressful method for the quilt. If the quilt is in a fairly clean condition, air the quilt in order to freshen it and avoid laundering.

Some quilts are musty and downright vile from decades of neglect. They must be cleaned in some way because they are simply too offensive in their present condition.

Ultimately, each quilt owner must make the decision and either accept the responsibility or sign away responsibility to someone else. Very few establishments will dry clean or wash a quilt for someone without a signed disclaimer.

## Washing Quilts

*"Q. How did you go about washing a quilt?"*

*"A. Well, it wasn't no easy job. We'd take and put them in a big tub of water and put in plenty of home-made soap and rub 'n rub. Then we'd lay them*

*out on a bench an' paddle 'em. Had a paddlin' stick,*
*they called it, and just come down with all the power*
*in both hands, and everywhere you struck that quilt*
*you'd make a clean place."* [43]

*"I washed it too—-washed it a lot, and most of*
*the time in Lye soap. Lye soap don't hurt a quilt*
*if the soap is made right."* [44]

# Quilt Cleaning Debate: Bathtub vs. Machine

## Bathtub

"It takes a weekend to wash one quilt properly, and it ties up a bathtub or a child's wading pool for much of that time."

"First immerse a clean light-colored sheet into the clean bathtub (with edges of the sheet draped over the sides of the tub), and then lower the quilt into the tub on top of the sheet in fan folds. . . .Such soaking can be done over a 12-hour period, with several changes of water. . . Leave the quilt to drain in the bathtub for several hours so the weight of the quilt will press out the excess water."  Nancy O'Bryant Puentes [45]

## Washing Machine

"Do not let excess water stay in fabric for any length of time. I use the washing machine as a vessel in which to wash my quilts.  I only allow the machine to gently agitate.  My main reason for placing a quilt in the machine is to spin the excess water out. If there are any fabrics that are likely to bleed, this will help prevent it since they will not stay excessively wet long enough to bleed onto adjacent fabrics.  Some people recommend washing quilts in a bathtub. I disagree.  Not only will the weight of all the water put a strain on the stitching when the quilt is lifted from the tub, but it is virtually impossible to get the excess water out of the quilt.  If any bleeding is likely to occur this will surely aid the process."  Jinny Beyer [46]

"Spinning will not harm the quilt–it is only centrifugal force, which is not agitating– and it is much easier on the fibers than handling a heavy dripping-wet quilt."  Quoting Harriet Hargrave, Greenbacker says she is the only one recommending gentle spin cycle. [47] Carol Wagner suggests washing the quilt in the bathtub and taking the wet quilt to the washing machine to drain the water out quickly. [48] Then again, Chloe LeMay, has no qualms about "putting them through my automatic washer and dryer. [49]

| Bathtub Method | Machine Method |
| --- | --- |
| Fill bathtub with water | Fill machine with water |
| Gentle handling | Lingerie cycle |
| Water drains naturally | Water drains without stress to fabric |
| Repeatedly rinse out soap | Rinsing out is less stressful due to gentle machine agitation |
| Remove wet quilt in a sheet and lay flat | Quilt has less water in it and fewer threads are likely to break |
| Messier | Easier |
| Never use dryer | Never use dryer |

Having used both methods for washing quilts, I find them equally effective. I like to soak a severely soiled quilt overnight and then drain the machine of soiled black water before refilling it and adding a cleaning soap. I find a bathtub difficult to use for this purpose.

Washing a badly soiled quilt takes a day whether you use the machine or the bathtub. Hand motion to loosen soil seems as stressful as a gentle lingerie cycle of agitation. Movement loosens debris and stains. So some agitation, whether by hand or machine, is necessary. Pretreatment of stains is possible with products listed below.

All experts recommend checking fabric for color fastness by rubbing a dry white cloth on the fabric. If cloth remains white, proceed by dampening white cloth in cold water and rubbing it on the fabric again. If cloth remains white, repeat the process with warm water; then finally repeat the process with the soap product to be used. Although these steps will help, fabric colors may still run in water once they are agitated.

Harriet Hargrave recommends a product called Easy Wash which helps remove bleeding color from a quilt. If this doesn't work, she recommends Snowy Bleach. The important factor is not to let the quilt dry once there has been bleeding of any kind. [50] If bleeding occurs, keep quilt wet and rinse repeatedly to lessen the chance of the color remaining in the adjoining fabrics. Once a quilt dries it is more difficult to remove the offending tint caused by bleeding.

# Stains

**Most often asked question:**
"Will this stain come out?"

**Best answer:**
"It depends."

## Dye Migration

Quilts and tops that have been folded and stored for decades often show dye migration. As the temperature and humidity fluctuated over the years, dyes were released from one area of the quilt to another. Brown stains that resemble furniture polish or rust are usually caused by dye migration over decades of intermittent heat and cold. Most stains caused by dye migration cannot be removed because the dye has permanently affixed itself to the adjoining fabric. Brown, black, red and yellow orange are the most notorious culprits.

*Major dye migration on large piece of unused fabric which was exposed to more than a century of extreme temperature fluctuations. Moisture followed by intense heat in yearly cycles may cause such severe dye migration. When seen on a small piece of fabric in a finished quilt, such dye migration is often mistaken for rust stain or spillage of some staining agent.*

*Minor dye migration on a pre-Civil War quilt. Often perceived as a rust stain, dye migration which happens over decades of heat and moisture changes, is usually permanent. More damage is done to quilts by owners trying to remove dye migration than in any other way. In trying to remove the "stain" they either do damage to the adjoining fabric or destroy the cotton fabric which has the stain.*

## Age Spots

Small brown spots, often called age spots by collectors, are caused by the oozing of oils from debris within the batting itself. All natural flecks of plant debris from the cotton can discharge a natural oily substance which discolors the fabric. Cotton seeds are not usually found in quilt batting because cotton seeds are the size of cherry pits and would not be left in a batting to be quilted. What is found in batting is plant debris which is not easily culled from the cotton fiber itself. Age spots are usually irreversible.

## Mildew

Mildew stains resemble small grey dots that grow in a speckled fashion across the fabric. At times, the dot clusters are thickly arranged; at other times, sparsely. Mildew stains come about after an extensive storing in a damp environment. Once the stains are embedded

there is little chance of their coming out, although they may be lightened enough to look like light shadowy spots. The odor of mildew is the first sign that the quilt should be removed from its environment and laundered as soon as possible to stop the ongoing spread.

According to the 1923 Butterick Dressmaking book, "Mildew is the hardest of all stains to remove, and can not all be taken out successfully. Salts of lemon or any of the mediums for ink and iron rust may be tried." [51]

## Water Stains

Water stains are difficult to remove fully if they have been on the fabric for a long period of time. When quilts have been stored for decades in an environment which becomes very moist, a natural water staining takes place. The most effective method to lighten a water stain is to use lemon juice, salt and sun.

Juice from a fresh lemon is to be squeezed over the stain. Salt is then sprinkled on top of the juice and the quilt is placed in the sun. After about an hour, rinse out the application. This process often needs to be repeated. For rinsing the treated area, the quilt may be placed over a large receptacle and secured with an elastic, so that hot water from a tea kettle can be poured through the treated area as if it were a sieve. Pat dry on both sides with absorbent towels and lay flat for drying. If the weather permits, the quilt may be dried outside, resting flat over adjoining chairs or on a screen. The screen must be covered with a sheet, and the quilt also covered with a sheet. This even air-drying will help the quilt to dry more quickly.

The method listed above is not only listed in *The Art of Dressmaking,* [52] but appears often among recipes for removing old stains from fragile fabrics. Patience is the key to its success because the process works slowly. The natural lemon juice treatment may be repeated as necessary. I have repeated the process seven or more times to lighten an age spot or mildew stain. Pick a sunny, out-of-the-way counter in your house or apartment for this project; it may require several days or weeks. Remember that the stains happened over time and stain removal takes time to be effective.

## Rust

Rust stains come out in one minute by using Whink Rust Stain Remover. If the stain does not come out in one minute, rinse immediately. This product has been very successfully used to remove large rust rings caused by bed springs. Whink, a poison, must be handled carefully with rubber gloves. Dye migration and blood-stains are often misread as rust stains and, for this reason, the manufacturer's guidelines must be carefully followed. If the stain is truly caused by rust, it will come out immediately. Whether the stain comes out or not, the quilt must be rinsed immediately and therefore the rinsing set-up must be ready prior to treatment.

## Blood

Blood responds well to stain treatment with lukewarm water and a product called New Again, available in the women's hygiene section of the supermarket. Place the quilt layer over a folded bath towel. Use a Q-tip applicator to dab a small amount of the New Again onto the blood stain and rub gently with the cotton applicator to loosen the blood. Rinse by applying a wet face cloth over the treated spot which is resting on the absorbent bath towel.

Repeatedly rinse that area only. An old time quilter said she places her quilt over a soup pot, takes a tea kettle of warm water and pours it directly over the area to be rinsed, and then she pats it dry between layers of toweling. This seems to be the most effective method of rinsing quickly.

Blood stains also respond well to pre-treatment with Clorox 2, or with a Q-tip application of diluted bleach. Again, caution needs to be used not to spread the bleach or New Again onto unstained fabric. Much damage can be caused to an entire quilt by flamboyant handling of a bleaching product. Patience is a key ingredient to any stain removal treatment.

## Grease

Powder or cornstarch will often draw grease stains out of fabric. Cover the stain with powder or cornstarch, place a piece of cotton over the powder and place a heavy book over this area. Let stand overnight before checking. The 1923 Butterick book suggests using brown wrapping paper and pressing over it with a hot iron: "The heat of the iron draws the grease from the material into the paper." [53] It's certainly worth a try.

## Filth

It's a terrible word, but filth is the best one to describe overall dirt and grime accumulated over decades. Soaking and draining, repeated over and over again, will do wonders for generic filth. The water will lighten with each rinsing, but it will start out to be black on the first few washings. At first, one thinks the dye is running, but it is actually the dirt and grime coming off. I surmise that part of the black is actually smoke soot deposits from the use of oil lamps and coal burners. The black color which comes out in the water can be frightening if one does not expect to see it arise from a multi-colored quilt. Finch and Putnam show glass jars of water holding rinse water at different stages from dark to light.

## Discoloration Due to Mouse Urine

Urine and uric acid were often used to set dyes into fabric. Sometimes fabrics which seem stained or bleach discolored are actually suffering from the release of their dyes because mice nesting in the folds of the quilt have left urine that unset the dyes. The discoloration may resemble a bleaching of the fabric.

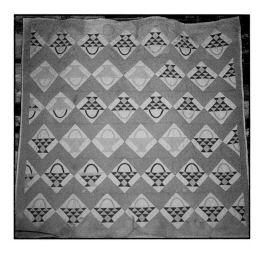

*Basket Quilt c. 1890. Classic example of fugitive dye. All baskets at one time were red and white; fugitive dyes created beige and white baskets that remain. (See page 103 for color).*

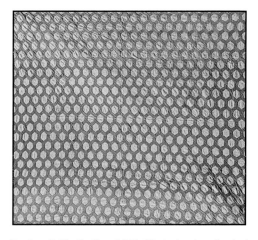

*Godey Design Cable Quilt c. 1850. Variation in color is due to fabric fading differently. Often such fading is unnoticed until the quilt is hung up.*

*Detail of Snow Flake Quilt. Lightening of green is due to unsetting of the dye by mouse urine. (See page 103 for color).*

## Fugitive Dyes

Some dyes are called fugitive because over time the original dye color mottles into various shades of the same color or at times disappears completely. Not all dyes were colorfast, and many home-dyed and manufactured fabrics discolored erratically.

If a fabric color has faded completely to another color, it is not seen as a stain, but if the fabric has only partially discolored, then the fugitive dye's mottled look can make the viewer think that someone has spilled a bleaching agent over the fabric. Brackman's color photo (page 60) shows the mottled look. Fugitive dye is perceived as a major problem if it is visually offensive but often goes unnoticed if it has occurred with regularity over an entire quilt.

*Products Used in Quilt Cleaning*

Ensure for quilts
Orvus Paste
Easy Wash
Snowy Bleach
Clorox 2
Ivory
Borax
Baking Soda
Lemon
Brown Octagon soap for
    pre-treatment of stains

Bleach in diluted form is praised by many collectors and dealers brave enough to launder their own quilts. Interestingly, the cleaning tips in the 1923 Butterick book include javelle water, which is a diluted bleach for cleaning many unwanted stains.

## After Washing

Once a quilt has been laundered, it should be laid out flat to dry. If you lay it outside, use a sheet under the quilt and a sheet above the quilt, so that no passing birds will add fresh stains to it. *Never hang a wet quilt on a clothes line!* When we see quilts hanging on clothes lines they are dry and being aired out. A wet cotton quilt hung on a clothes line will dry in a warped fashion and the weight of the wet cotton will break quilting threads and seams.

*Never place a wet quilt in a dryer;* the wet quilt will puncture holes through the fabric. A wad of cotton in a loosely quilted piece will have the approximate weight of a small lime and for this reason the weight of the wet cotton will pummel itself against the more fragile fabric and quite literally punch holes in it.

Allow the quilt enough time to dry prior to storing it or it will get mildewed in storage. The outer layers dry first, so that a quilt that feels dry may still be quite damp inside. If the quilt is to be stored, keep it out in a cool dry place for at least a week before storing it. This will guarantee that the inside is as dry as the outside.

## Vacuuming

Fragile quilts, both cotton and silk, can be vacuumed to remove surface dirt which might damage the textile. Penny McMorris and Nancy O'Bryant Puentes both suggest covering the quilt with a piece of screening to protect the fibers. Fiberglas coated windowscreening is available by the foot in most hardware stores and a piece of masking tape or duct tape should be folded over the edges of the screen to protect the quilt from being caught by the raw edges of the screen. A low powered vacuum should be used and if the quilt is extremely fragile, it is recommended that the nozzle be kept a half inch or more above the surface of the quilt. [54]

## Storing

Quilts like to be treated like people. They like environments that are just right. They like to breathe and want no severe extremes in temperature or humidity. Rather than being put away in attics, cellars or garages, quilts like to be treated as welcome house guests. Store them (if necessary) where they can be guaranteed even temperature and humidity.

Fluctuations in heat, cold and humidity are the main causes of fabric deterioration; they can rob cotton fiber of half its tensile strength. This process, called tendering, reduces even the finest cotton to a paper-like substance. If the fabric is allowed to tender over decades, it can be reduced to a powdery-like paper that crumbles at our touch.

## Acid Free Paper

Acid free paper is ideal for wrapping and storing quilts. Used between the layers to prevent dye migration and stress, it serves as a non-toxic buffer for the layers of the quilt. Available through many catalogues, acid free paper is now quite easy to acquire.

## Roll, Don't Fold

If a quilt is repeatedly folded in the same manner, the exposed sides of the fold discolor and disintegrate with exposure to extremes in temperature. This folding of quilts over decades has caused major damage and discoloration to the most spectacular quilts. Damage along the fold line cannot be reversed.

When storing a quilt, flip-flop it into thirds or fifths, inserting acid-free paper within the folds. Some collectors advise bunching up the acid free paper to create a soft curve of poof to pad the quilt from further stress. A gentle rolling of a quilt, like a sleeping bag is recommended for all quilts. Most of us have been trained to fold and fold neatly and flat. We must remind ourselves not to fold a quilt.

## Cotton Sheeting

Cotton pillowcases or sheets are ideal for storing quilts because they allow the quilt fabric to breathe. Any piece of 100% cotton may be used to cover a quilt once it has been protected with acid free paper.

## Avoid Wood

Avoid direct contact with wood so that no oil will transfer through the sheeting to the quilt. Wood breathes with the seasons and, like all natural substances, it exudes its inner oils with time. If you must place the prepared quilt on a wooden surface, place a piece of plastic or wax paper between the wood and the cotton cover.

## Keep Out of Direct Sunlight

This may sound too silly to say. However, sunlight doesn't remain in the same location throughout the day. A quilt stored in an under-bed storage box may get late afternoon sun in that location day after day and when removed may be alarmingly discolored. Because we are not in the same room at different times of the day, we may not think a particular spot is sunny when, in fact, it is. Make sure you pick a storage spot out of all direct sunlight.

Never store a quilt in a plastic bag. It will mildew. Always ship a quilt in a plastic bag to protect it during the trip only.

## Shipping

Hundreds of quilts are shipped across the country every day because of antique shows and quilt shows. Of the thousands of quilts that have been shipped in and out of our studio over a decade, not one has been lost in transit. If a quilt is to be shipped for any purpose, the following guidelines are helpful.

❦ Always ship in a plastic bag which is well sealed. This will protect the quilt from possible spillage from other containers.

❦ A separate address label should be included inside the bag with a phone number of the person to call in case the box is damaged.

❦ A recipient should be designated because an unattended box could either be stolen or destroyed by a family pet. One quilt was gnawed by a family dog chained outside, and the quilt recipient had to make full restitution for the quilt shipped on speculation.

❦ Insure a quilt properly. Although insurance costs a bit more, it is worth the peace of mind. United Parcel Service insures up to $25,000 for any one item.

❦ Take a photo before shipping a quilt. This precaution will be needed to process any insurance claim.

❦ A written appraisal is recommended prior to shipping a quilt. Although a good photo will show what the quilt looked like, a written description and estimate is further proof of the quilt's existence. Quilt shipments are not usually picked for insurance scams, but insurance is not automatically guaranteed without validation by the sender.

❦ To make sure a quilt has arrived, enclose a SASE for mailing back a receipt to you.

❦ If the quilt is to be in a quilt show, enclose hanging instructions for show and prepare a label with all necessary information that can be attached to the back of the quilt. A piece of muslin may be folded over and sewn together; the name, address, phone number, dimensions, name of quilt design may be inked or typed onto the muslin. The muslin square can then be hand sewn onto the back of the quilt.

# Hanging

The least stressful way to hang a quilt is to distribute the weight evenly across its width.

First decide which side will be treated as the top. Although this sounds too mundane to mention, most quilts have a top or bottom which is not always readily apparent. Often a square quilt will have such dominant colors on one side that this side needs to be treated as a top or bottom in order not to make the quilt look lopsided. We are trained to read from left to right and from top to bottom. This visual training extends to our walls. Before hanging a quilt permanently, have friends hold it up so that all four choices can be seen from a distance. Keep repeating this process until you are sure of which way is the top for you.

Although choosing which side will be the top of the quilt is a personal choice, the size of the room and the walls are also considerations. If the quilt is to hang on a 15-foot-high wall, any damage would be less pronounced at the top, because the eye will scan from top to bottom and minimize the impact of the uppermost part of the quilt.

If the quilt is to be hung on an 8-foot-high wall, and other furniture is in front of the quilt, any damage should be toward the bottom of the quilt, where it will be visually minimized. Hanging a quilt is a process more than an event. Sometimes, after living with a quilt, one realizes it should hang in another direction.

A square set on a wall as a diamond may add a dramatic impact to an otherwise ordinary quilt. For hanging in the diamond position a quilt should not only be square, but strong enough in design or color to hold its own on a large wall space. An oversized stretcher form may be the best choice for this kind of display.

❧ Soft curtain tapes used for pinch pleat drapes may also be cut to size and sewn onto the back of the quilt.

❧ Wide grosgrain ribbon is also a good choice for hand sewing a sleeve.

❧ If one does not sew at all and wishes to create a sleeve, rustproof safety pins may be evenly pinned along the back side of a quilt for a temporary display. If the quilt is to be displayed for any extended period of time, a hand sewn sleeve is desirable.

*HAND SEWN CASING*

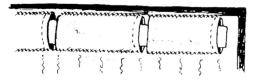

*Open sections may be created for wall supports on larger quilt to be displayed.*

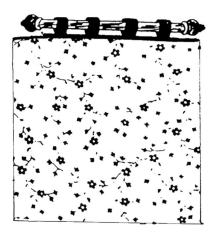

*Tabs are created in the same way as tab curtains. Tabs may be directly applied to the quilt if it is very sturdy and relatively new. Older quilts should have tabs applied to a conventional sleeve and entire sleeve-with-tabs may then be hand sewn to the back of the quilt as in illustration.*

Hand sew a sleeve casing just below the binding. Make casing a generous 4" to 5" to allow the rod and fixtures to be hidden behind the quilt.

## Here are various choices for sleeve casings:

❧ 100% cotton folded over twice and sewn into a tube.

## Tapestry Look

Tabs can be made using directions for making tab curtains. Once tabs are cut to a uniform size, they can be machine stabilized on a twill tape, grosgrain ribbon or muslin sleeve before they are hand sewn onto the back of a quilt. Tabs are very effective if the rod is an important part of the total look. When a decorative rod is used to display a quilt, tabs will add drama to the hanging. This is particularly true for Crazy Quilts displayed on lavish brass or antique rods with ornamental finials. This hanging technique resembles that used for hand-loomed tapestries from earlier centuries.

Some quilt shops have custom made wooden shelves that are designed to clamp a quilt into place. This method can be effective in a country decor, but would seem out of place in a modern apartment or house.

Tracy Jamar offers a unique hanging system which is adjustable for different textile presentations, and Pie Galinat also offers custom designed frames for quilt display. (See Resources.) Framing is a definite consideration for smaller pieces. If a smaller quilt or quilt fragment is to be framed, make sure that the frame shop will follow textile guidelines that allow the quilt to breathe within the glass frame. Also, acid-free paper must be used so that the textile does not lie directly against wood which could eventually discolor and destroy the fabric.

Stretching a quilt or quilt fragment over a stretcher frame—like a painter's canvas—gives dramatic control over the shape of the quilt. Two methods most often used for this purpose are to apply the quilt to a cotton backing which will be stretched, or to apply cotton piece to the quilt fragment which will then be stretched.

According to Bishop, the best method for displaying a quilt is to reback it with new fabric, leaving several inches overlapping on each edge. Then the quilt can be stretched over a wooden frame, much like the canvas of an oil painting. Although expensive, this technique distributes the weight evenly and the frame may be turned and hung four different ways,

insuring that the weight of the textile will not be concentrated on only one side. [55] Although this technique requires a large wall space, it does minimize the stress on any one side and would be ideal for hanging a smaller square quilt on the diamond as mentioned above.

## Velcro

Avoid using Velcro to mount quilts. Although some people get good results fastening a quilt to a board with Velcro, we have seen too much universal damage from this adhesive.

The problem is not the product itself, which is very effective for hanging textile. People are the problem with Velcro mounts. They peel off the textile as if they were pulling off a Bandaid from an arm. Velcro wants to be yanked. By its very nature, Velcro is a strong adhesive tape, which requires strong pulling to be removed. When Velcro-finished quilts are pulled from the receiving board, the fragile quilt fabric too often is severely damaged.

If one must use Velcro, Mary O'Bryant Puentes' method seems the most gentle to the textile. One Velcro side is attached to a separate strip of cotton and the cotton band is hand-appliqued to the quilt. Puentes recommends that every few stitches, one stitch is brought through all the quilt layers so as not to stress the back of the quilt exclusively. Putnam and Finch have wonderful photos of this technique in all of the stages. [56] If this is done in such a way that it doesn't show or doesn't pucker the front of the quilt, the method is quite acceptable. The second scratchy side of the Velcro is attached to a board or stretcher frame made to size and stapled into place. The quilt is then mounted onto the prepared frame.

Velcro should never be sewn directly to a quilt back or it will always pull at the backing and will often rip the cotton quilt fabric which cannot accept the full force of Velcro removal.

*APPLICATION OF ALL CASINGS.*
*Cotton casing is hand sewn to quilt.*

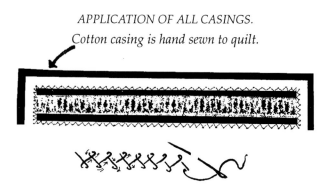

*Hand stitch recommended for application.*

*All experts recommend that every 5 to 8 stitches, a stitch should penetrate all three layers of the quilt in order to ease the stress placed on the back of the quilt.*

## Scallop Edge Quilts

Rings may be hand sewn to the end of a scallop or swag border. If the scallop or swag is gentle or in close repeats, these hand sewn rings will be enough to hold the quilt on the rod. The rod will show in between the scallop or swag, so a compatible color should be chosen. Plexirods are also available through specialty shops and may be right for the quilt.

Hand sewn tabs made of cloth may also be evenly applied to each swag or scallop. Grosgrain ribbon is a good choice for this project. If the scallop or swag is quite wide, two or three rings or tabs will be needed to support the weight. Measure precisely so that all rings or tabs are positioned identically.

*RINGS ADDED TO TOP OF SCALLOPS FOR SUPPORT*

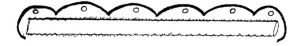

Keep in mind that rings flop up with tension, therefore they should be positioned so as to be invisible when they carry the weight of the rod. With a large quilt that has a swag or scallop border, a casing may be added below the swag or scallop to carry the majority of the weight of the quilt, and rings or tabs may be sewn by hand to carry the weight of the swag or scallop only.

## Quilts that Ripple When Hanging

When a quilt does not hang straight because the sides have been stretched differently over the decades, a second casing may be added to the bottom of the quilt so that a dowel or flattened rod can be inserted for weight. This additional weighted sleeve at the bottom usually solves the problem.

## Fading Sunlight

Quilts do fade in sunlight. No one can change this fact. Whether it is on a bed, a wall or a stair landing, a quilt that repeatedly gets direct sunlight will fade. The question to ask is whether one would rather live with quilts or tuck them away. Living with quilts on walls or beds means they will age just like humans. A question to verbalize is: Does the human own the quilt or does the quilt own the human?

Hanging a quilt on a wall causes less stress and less friction to the quilt fabric than using it on a bed. While the quilt will receive less abuse from handling it also will give more daily pleasure to the viewer.

## Cleaning a Wall Quilt

Vacuuming a quilt is a very effective way to clean off everyday dust which does accumulate. Just as one would vacuum a drapery or a lampshade, so can one vacuum a hanging quilt.

## Framing

Quilts need to breathe even in a frame. Sunlight also penetrates regular plate glass. Several textile conservators, in working with framing

concerns, have devised a special method as well as materials to be used in museum quality framing. (See Resources.)

A family heirloom is best framed by an expert who will be concerned with its preservation. Textiles need to breathe even in frames and acid free mountings are recommended. Do ask many questions, and do your research before having any textile framed.

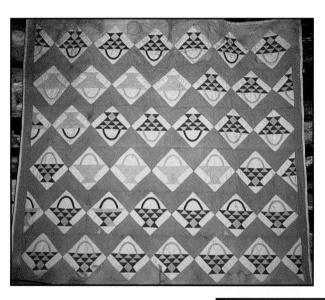

*Classic example of fugitive dye. All baskets at one time were red and white.*

*The unsetting of the green dye was caused by mice.*

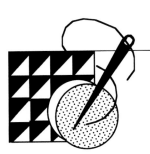

# 10

# Resources

## Ordering by Mail

THE SUPPLIERS LISTED HERE ship to all parts of the country–as well as all over the world. Speedy and helpful, they fill orders, usually within 48 hours of receiving them. And they generally accept major credit cards.

Retail ordering, I have found, is preferable to wholesale ordering because most amounts required for restoration work are less than bolt or case size. For paying a higher price, one saves on storage and gains diversity.

A major rule to follow in ordering fabrics is to order generous yardage if it is a fabric which you truly love. For example, if you plan on restoring distressed 1920–40 quilts and you find a particular reproduction excellent for your needs, consider buying three to nine yards or more. Some fabrics are produced for a four-month sales period and will no longer be available in six months.

Once catalogues have been received, I find it helpful to keep them in a separate file and keep lists of products bought. When ordering I keep information together for further reference. If I have ordered a product, sight unseen, such as a new batting, I keep a sample of it in the file.

I have used all of the catalogues listed below and have found the people on the phone most willing to help. But words alone cannot

*Sample sheet taken from workbook. Concrete reference sheets are like cloth recipes to be referred to at any future time. The more detailed and precise for the restorer, the more helpful the sample sheets will be for later reference.*

adequately describe fabric, no matter how hard one tries. It is necessary to order swatches or to mail a swatch to be matched. Many order forms have a second choice column, a substitute column and a backorder column. Although mail order will never appease the need to see and touch the fabric in real life, it is certainly easier than traveling hundreds of miles in ten directions trying to find exact matches.

Many quilt and fabric stores carry the products needed. Definitely check out all the shops in your area first, because it will be better to see the fabric, batting or product if you can. If you want to purchase a large amount of a particular product, many shop owners will be willing to order for you, but they face the same problem we do here at the studio. To order wholesale, one must order a bolt, case, dozen, etc. of the product through a distributor, and this requires a firm knowledge that a large amount of this product is going to sell.

Once a commitment is made to X amount of yardage, there is a major responsibility to follow through. Our shop has been badly hurt by customers who absolutely wanted a particular product in volume, and then when notified of its arrival said they had purchased the product someplace else. The shop owner cannot return an order simply because the customer changed his/her mind. If you feel strongly about having your local quilt or fabric shop do a special order for you, you may wish to make a commitment deposit.

# Fabric by Mail Order

### The Patchworks
6676 Amsterdam Road
Manhattan, MT 59741
Phone: 1-406-282-7218, Dept. Z

Margo Krager specializes in reproduction fabrics and carries more than 600 bolts of reproduction prints. Pre-1900 print reproductions are not as easy to find as pastel reproductions. If you are working on a particular quilt, send a color photo along for matching. Margo has recently added authentic shirting fabric and real flour sacking fabric.

### Keepsake Quilting
Route 25, P.O. Box 1618
Centre Harbor, NH 03226-1618
Phone: 1-603-253-8731
FAX: 603-253-8346

For overall mail ordering of all kinds of quilting supplies, this is armchair shopping at its best. More than 600 swatches are available. I order a great deal through Keepsake because they are fast, personable and stock many different sizes of battings and backing fabrics. No one quilt shop can offer such diversity without a huge overhead, and most quilt restoration projects, as we know, do not require bolts and cases. Acid free paper and plastic products are also available.

### The Ultimate Quilting Outlet
6700 West 44th Avenue
P.O. Box 394
Wheat Ridge, CO 80034-0394
Phone: 1-303-420-4272, ext. 100
FAX: 303-420-7358

This catalogue has wonderful color photos of fabrics which give a clear idea of what the buyer is selecting. Also other quilting supplies. *Quilter's Newsletter Magazine* often carries large and colorful ads of special products available through Quilts and Other Comforts which is associated with The Ultimate Quilting Outlet. If you see something you want, order rather quickly; their large audience buys fast.

### Cabin Fever Calico
P.O. Box 550106
Atlanta, GA 30355-2506
Phone: 1-800-762-2246

Cabin Fever offers a wide selection of solid

100% cotton fabrics as well as diverse quilting supplies in their catalogue.

## Vintage Fabric

**Kirk Collection**
1513 Military Avenue
Omaha, NE 68111
Phone: 1-800-398-2542
          1-412-551-0386

Here you can find over 10,000 yards of vintage fabrics at any given time. Sounds unbelievable! Nancy Kirk takes a personal interest in helping you. The Kirk Collection grew out of the Kirks' purchase of the Warner Brothers Period Fabric and Trim Collection. They keep adding to it. Be specific about your needs and send samples for matches.

**Northampton Fabric Co.**
150 Main Street
Northampton, MA 01060
Phone: 1-413-585-0305

The staff will happily assist you with vintage fabrics, laces, trims, linens and fringe. The Northampton Bead Company is just next door and sells early specialty beads and buttons. Northampton Fabric Company opened in June 1993.

**Shirley McElderry**
Route 6, Box 277
Ottumwa, IA 52501
Phone: 1-515-684-7483

Shirley McElderry will help quilters in any fabric search. Send a swatch along with the dimensions of the piece you need.

**Georgina B. Fries**
P.O. Box 6
Lothian, MD 20711
Phone: 1-301-867-0665

Georgina Fries lectures on the topic, "New Quilts from Old", and has an extensive collection of old quilts, tops and fabrics which she is willing to share with others in need of finding just the right match for a particular restoration.

**Claire McKarns**
3461 Buman Road
Encinitas, CA 92024
Phone: 1-619-756-5718
FAX: 1-619-756-4989

Claire McKarns has an extensive collection of vintage fabrics and is willing to help others fabric-match. Send swatch along with the amount of fabric needed.

**Nancy Reese**
P.O. Box 551
Adamstown, PA 19501
Phone: 1-215-484-4659
          *or*
**Renninger's Antique Market**
2500 N. Redding Road
Denver, PA 17517
Phone: 1-215-267-2177
(Sunday 7:30 AM to 5:00 PM)

Nancy sells antique fabrics at both places. Many buyers and dealers rent and sell at Renninger's.

**Diane Reese Antique Textiles**
P.O. Box 598
Townsend, MA 01469
Phone: 1-508-597-5149

Diane specializes in antique fabrics and has a generous supply of yardage as well as quilt tops and squares to offer.

**Schmul Meier, Inc.**
23 Main Street
Tarrytown, NY 10591
Phone: 1-914-332-1310
Thurs.-Sat.
or
328 East 59th St., Suite 4
New York, NY 10022
Phone: 1-212-644-8590
Tues.–Fri.

Schmul Meier specializes in European fabrics. Though the firm does not specialize in fabric matching, if you needed a larger piece of rare fabric, they could be the perfect source for old velvet, silk or English and French pre-Civil War cottons.

### Other Vintage Fabric Sources

Many quilt dealers offer vintage fabrics along with fabric squares. Tied quilts with some damage and discarded clothing from the 19th century through the Depression all offer pieces of fabric from the past.

# Embroidery Threads

## Silk Threads

**Madeira Marketing LTD**
600 East 9th St., 3rd Floor
Michigan City, IN 46360
Phone: 1-219-873-1000
FAX: 1-219-879-6181
    104 colors

**YLI Corporation**
P.O. Box 109
482 N. Freedom Blvd.
Provo, UT 84601
Inquiries: 1-801-377-3900
Orders: 1-800-854-1932
FAX: 1-801-375-2879
    211 colors

**LACIS**
3163 Adeline Street
Berkeley, CA 94703
Phone: 1-510-843-7178
FAX: 1-510-843-5018

## Cotton Threads

**Herrschners**
Hoover Road
Stevens Point, WI 54492
Phone: 1-800-441-0838
FAX: 1-715-341-2250
Customer Service/Info: 1-715-341-0560

DMC cotton perle and threads for tying quilts in a rainbow array.

**National Thread & Supply Co.**
695 Red Oak Road
Stockbridge, GA 30281
Phone: 1-800-331-7600
FAX: 1-404-389-9115

## General Sewing Needs

**Clotilde, Inc.**
2 Sew Smart Way B8031
Stevens Point, WI 54481-8031
Phone Orders: 1-800-772-2891
Customer Service: 1-800-545-4002
FAX: 1-715-341-3082

This catalogue is a sewer's delight and has greatly expanded its quilt supplies over the last five years. Many of the different restoration tools, the ironing hams and small pressing boards are available. Catalogue supplies are for sewing, quilting, needlework and crafts, including such products as fusing webs, acid free paper, Fray Check, Seams Great.

## Custom Dyeing of Fabric

**True Colors**
R.D. 3, Box 91, Wood Road
Pittstown, NJ 08867
Phone: 1-908-730-7398

Carol Esch is able to successfully match your desired color in 100% cotton. These hand dyed fabrics are especially useful when rebinding or reconstructing two-color quilts whose solid colors have faded over the decades.

## Fading Kits

**By Jupiter**
6801 N. 21st Ave., Suite 0
Phoenix, AZ 85015
Phone: 1-800-242-2574

Mary Maison devised her Quilt Fading kit while searching for faded old fabric in her own quilt restoration projects.

## Tools

**Micro-Mark**
340 Snyder Avenue
Berkeley Heights, NJ 07922-1595
Phone: 1-800-225-1066
FAX: 1-908-665-9383
Outside USA: 1-908-464-6764

This small tools catalogue carries the surgeon's quick release clamping tool and the crocodile-action ear polypus, a surgical instrument designed to pass through a ⅛" hole and still open and close its jaws. The polypus can place or retrieve micro-size objects. Although many of the tools are intended for building miniatures, some are just right for hard to reach sections in quilt restorations.

## Books

**Dover Street Booksellers, LTD.**
8673 Commerce Drive #13
P.O. Box 1563
Easton, MD 21601
Phone: 1-800-235-5358
Customer Service/Info: 1-410-822-9329

Nan Scholley not only carries over 700 titles on quilting, but will also help quilters locate books which may not be listed in her extensive catalogue.

**American Quilter's Society**
P.O. Box 3290
Paducah, KY 42002-3290
Phone: 1-800-626-5420
FAX: 1-502-898-8890

**Books Unlimited (ASN)**
Division School of Needlework
1455 Linda Vista Drive
San Marcos, CA 92069
Phone: 1-619-471-2320

**Craftsman's Touch**
812 Beltrami Ave.
Bemidji, MN 56601

**Dicmar Trading Co.**
8850 Brookville Rd.
Silver Spring, MD 20910
Phone: 1-301-585-4320

**Joslin Hall Rare Books**
**on Textiles & Fashion**
P.O. Box 516
Concord, MA 01742
Phone: 1-508-371-3101

**LACIS**
(See Threads above for address)

LACIS has hundreds of textile books in specialty areas and carries both the *Mender's Manual* and *The Care and Preservation of Textiles*. Order their catalogue for the complete listing.

**Quilters' Resource, Inc.**
2211 N. Elston
P.O. Box 148850
Chicago, IL 60614
Phone: 1-312-278-5695

**Sabanek Associates**
Rt. 25
P.O. Box 1618
Centre Harbor, NH 03226-1618
Phone: 1-603-253-8346

**Vermont Patchworks**
229 Old Plymouth Rd.
Box 229
Shrewsbury, VT 05738
Phone: 1-802-492-3590

# *Batting*

Batting is generally a personal choice for quilters. Most companies will send small samples with a SASE, some without. Better to include. Experiment with different battings to get the results wanted. Again, keeping a sample file is an excellent way to keep track of which battings act which way.

**Fairfield Processing Corp.**
P.O. Box 1157
Danbury, CT 06813-1157
Phone: 1-800-243-0989
FAX: 1-203-792-9710

**Hobbs Bonded Fibers**
P.O. Box 3000
Mexia, TX 76667
Phone: 1-817-729-3223

**Liebhardt Mills, Inc.**
9100 S. County Road, 800 West
Daleville, IN 47334
Phone: 1-317-378-6500

**Taylor Bedding**
Fiber & Quilted Products
P.O. Box 979
Taylor, TX 76574-0979
Phone: 1-800-234-9105

**Warm Products, Inc.**
161100 Woodinville-Redmond Road, #4
Woodinville, WA 98072
Phone: 1-800-234-WARM
FAX: 1-206-488-2611

## Specialty Battings

**Taos Mountain Wool Works**
P.O. Box 327
Arroyo Hondo, NM 87513
Phone: 1-505-776-2925

**Letty's Own**
RR 2
10 Wadman Road
Hillsdale, NY 12529
Phone: 1-518-325-5531

Letty Malin grows her own Cheviot's lamb's wool and has it professionally batted after each shearing. Like Letty, you may have wool growers and spinners in your own area who can supply freshly processed wool for restoration of quilts.

**Silk Batting** is available through YLI Corp. (listed above under Threads).

## Special Products

### Acid Free Paper

All quilting and sewing catalogues listed above sell acid free paper. LACIS offers a full range of conservation supplies.

### Plastic

Often called mylar or stenciling and template sheets, various kinds of plastic see-through sheets are available through Keepsake Quilting and Quilts and Other Comforts (see above).

### Hams

Available through Clotilde catalogue and at most sewing stores.

### Fusing Web

Most sewing stores carry a full line of fusing webs and bonded interfacings in various grades, thicknesses and colors. Ask, look, feel. LACIS carries So Sheer Fusible Knit.

### Dental Tools & Long Tweezer

Both Clotilde's and Micro-Mark catalogues offer these long handled tools for various projects.

### Crepeline

**Jean Lyle**
Box 289
Quincy, IL 62306
Phone: 1-217-222-8910

LACIS carries this as Crepeline in their catalogue.

# Quilt Conservation and Restoration Services

Seeking professional help in restoring an antique quilt is a process. Prior to sending a family quilt, write for more information or call to ask questions. Estimates cannot be given over the phone. Some studios charge to assess the project; others don't. Some studios send out the quilt to be worked on elsewhere; others do all work within their studios. References and recommendations from other quilt galleries and collectors help each quilt owner to choose which studio or methods are best for his/her quilt.

## Quilt Conservation

Quilt conservationists use strict rules and procedures in handling antique textiles. Conservation methods require equipped studios or access to such studios. The locations listed below fall into this category. Any quilt believed to be of rare value would require the assistance of a textile conservator for the continued preservation of a rare and important historical textile.

**Textile Conservation Workshop, Inc.**
Main Street
South Salem, NY 10590
Phone: 1-914-763-5805

Patsy Orlofsky is the executive director of the Textile Conservation Workshop which was founded in 1978 to act as a new conservation resource for museums, historic agencies and private individuals.

**Textile/Costume Conservation**
**& Aesthetic Services**
579 17th Street
Brooklyn, NY 11218
Phone: 1-718-788-1211

Consulting conservator at the Museum of American Folk Art, Gina Bianco, offers a decade of conservation experience as partner and chief conservator of the former Helene Von Rosenstiel, Inc.

**Margaret Geiss-Mooney:**
Textile Conservator
1124 Celia Court
Petaluma, CA 94952
Phone: 1-707-763-8694

With a degree in textile science and conservation equipment, Margaret Geiss-Mooney has worked on quilts for the last 15 years.

**Textile Conservation Center**
Museum of American Textile History
800 Massachusetts Avenue
North Andover, MA 01845
Phone: 1-508-686-0191

The chief conservator, Kathy Francis, works closely with all projects and will guide anyone in need of more information.

**LACIS Studio**
3163 Adeline Street
Berkeley, CA 94703
Phone: 1-510-843-7178
FAX: 1-510-843-5018

As recognized experts in the field of lace, Kaethe and Jules Kliot direct a separate studio for the restoration, preservation and collection of antique laces and other textiles. LACIS offers a repair service for fine textiles, garments and beadwork.

## Quilt Restoration

Quilt restorers are listed by state to simplify the reader's search for the nearest quilt restorer. All the quilt restorers listed below ask that they be contacted by phone first. Most quilt restorers have home studios and need to meet with clients by private appointment only. <u>Quilts should never be shipped without prior approval of the quilt restorer.</u> If one is concerned with the quality of quilt restoration, references may be the best reassurance because most quilts, once restored, are returned to their owners. Just as a stained glass restorer would refer you to previous restorations, so also must a quilt restorer refer interested clients to previous quilt restorations. No doubt, fine quilt restorers have been omitted from the list below. Many quilt restorers do not advertise in national publications and are, at this time, difficult to locate. If you are a quilt restorer and would like to be included in any future listing, please send me your name and number.

I have spoken with all of the quilt restorers listed here. They are a professional and knowledgeable group of women who bring a vast expertise to their art. When I began writing this book, I thought very few people were involved in this field. In two years I discovered that I am in good company and that quilt restoration is alive and well across the country. Here, by state, are those I interviewed:

## California

**Susan Bradford**
c/o Sawtooth Quilt Shop
1560 Fourth Street
San Rafael, CA 94901
Phone: 1-415-453-1711

Susan Bradford has been restoring quilts for 13 years and teaching quilt making at her studio location.

**Diane E. Ferguson**
2526 Royal Crest Drive
Escondido, CA 92025

Phone: 1-619-735-9119
Diane Ferguson has been a quilt restorer for a decade.

**Caroline Lieberman**
55 Arroyo Way
San Francisco, CA 94127
Phone: 1-415-584-3794

A quilting teacher for 20 years and a quilt restorer for 14 years, Caroline Lieberman teaches quilt restoration techniques for bindings, edges and finishings.

**Claire McKarns**
3461 Buman Road
Encinitas, CA 92024
Phone: 1-619-756-5718
FAX: 1-619-756-4989

Claire McKarns has been restoring quilts for more than five years and also has an extensive vintage fabric collection from which to choose.

**Caroline Strauch**
3681 West Country Club Lane
Sacramento, CA 95821
Phone: 1-916-485-9593

Caroline Strauch has restored quilts for eight years and applies both restoration and conservation methods at her studio.

**Susie Wright**
3327 Calavo Drive
Spring Valley, CA 91978
Phone: 1-619-660-2099

Susie Wright has restored quilts for five years.

**Manuela Yokota**
24251 Cherry Hills Place
Laguna Niguel, CA 92677
Phone: 1-714-495-4777

Manuela Yokota has been restoring quilts for west coast collectors for nine years.

*Colorado*

**Annabelle Kimball**
9927 West 87th Avenue
Arvada, CO 80005
Phone: 1- 303-425-6969

Annabelle Kimball brings 20 years of experience to repairing antique quilts. Originally from Pennsylvania, Annabelle ran a quilt shop in Taos, NM before moving to Colorado.

**Rocky Mountain Quilts**
Betsey Telford
3847 Alt 6 & 24
Palisade, CO 81526
Phone: 1-800-464-0833

"Our restoration business has become a thriving cottage industry," says Betsey, "with women in Colorado, Texas, Arkansas and Oklahoma restoring quilts and linens for us."

*Connecticut*

**Susan Hendrick Wilson**
370 Whitney Avenue
Trumbull, CT 06611
Phone: 1-203-268-1321

Susan Hendrick Wilson has been repairing antique quilts for 15 years and brings great textile knowledge to each project.

**Patti Schmer**
Antiques Flora
Cornwall Bridge Railroad Station
Cornwall, CT 06754
Phone: 1-203-672-0381

Patti restores antique quilts from her antique shop located in western Connecticut.

*Florida*

**Pamela Pampe**
10383 SW 116th Street
Miami, FL 33176
Phone: 1-305-251-2648

Pamela Pampe teaches quilt restoration and conservation techniques in the Miami area.

*Iowa*

**Shirley McElderry**
Route 6, Box 277
Ottumwa, IA 52501
Phone: 1-515-684-7483

Shirley McElderry has been restoring antique quilts for ten years and is willing to help network with other quilters in finding the perfect match. Shirley's article, "Repairing Older Quilts and Tops," appeared in *American Quilter,* Spring, 1992.

*Kentucky*

**Kathryn Steed**
5508 Russell Cave Road
Lexington, KY 40511
Phone: 1-606-299-8921

Kathryn has been restoring quilts for a decade.

## Maine

**Kate Adams Designs**
P.O. Box 3025
Kennebunkport, ME 04046
Phone: 1-800-553-3766

Kate Adams creates miniatures that are exact reproductions of traditional patterns. If all you have left of a quilt are very small pieces, you may consider having her reproduce the quilt within a framed miniature.

**Nancy Ward Castonia**
186 Middle Road
Cumberland Center, ME 04021
Phone: 1-207-829-5803

Nancy Castonia has restored quilts for the last five years. As a miniature quilt artist, Nancy will also reproduce a favorite family quilt from the fabrics in the original quilt.

## Michigan

**Delores Bullock**
1514 Red Run Drive
Royal Oak, MI 48073
Phone: 1-313-545-5484

Delores Bullock is knowledgeable in quilt history through her museum work and conserves and preserves antique quilts.

**Laura Rodin**
15700 Windmill Pointe Drive
Grosse Pointe, MI 48230
Phone: 1-313-822-2311

Laura Rodin has been restoring quilts for seven years.

## Missouri

**Quilt Restoration Specialists**
333 North Ash Street
Webb City, MO 64870
Phone: 1-417-782-2903  Jack Waggener
Phone: 1-417-673-2200  Betty Bridges

A seamstress for 25 years, Betty has 14 years experience as a quilter and teacher prior to restoring quilts with Jack Waggener, a dealer who has an eye for fine antique quilts.

## New Jersey

**Kathy Siegrist**
6 Wood Dale Court
Sussex, NJ 07461
Phone: 1-201-875-8215

Kathy Siegrist enjoys hand quilting a finished top.

## New York

**Mary Lou Alexander**
2269 Trimble Road
Ontario, NY 14519
Phone: 1-315-524-9083

Mary Lou Alexander has restored quilts for the last ten years and has lectured on quilt restoration at quilt guilds in the Rochester area.

**Pie Galinat**
Phone: 1-212-741-3259

Pie Galinat, who requested that her address not be given, has restored quilts for 18 years. Working from an extensive library of vintage fabrics, she also offers custom frame service designed for textiles.

**Betty LaCasse**
37 Prescott Avenue
White Plains, NY 10605
Phone: 1-914-948-7573

Betty LaCasse specializes in invisible repair of all textiles, from cashmere and linen to reconstruction of antique lace. With over 40 years of experience, Betty is recommended by several textile museums and has been featured in national publications.

**Jamar Textile Restorations**
250 Riverside Drive
New York, NY 10025
Phone: 1-212-866-6426

Tracy Jamar has been restoring quilts for more than 14 years. She also sells Walker Systems, a new line of textile hanging devices she invented with her father, Walker Jamar.

**K & K Quilteds**
P.O. Box 23, Route 23
Hillsdale, NY 12529
Phone: 1-518-325-4502

K & K Quilteds is an eight-room quilt restoration studio which houses ten walls of coded vintage fabrics. Kittie James Becker and Camille Dalphond Cognac (Kami) have restored quilts for 12 years. They have a national networking with vintage fabric collectors throughout the country. All of the techniques described in this book were used, and many of them devised, at their studio.

**Robin Greeson Textile Restoration**
Box 276, Snydertown Road
Craryville, NY 12521
Phone: 1-518-851-7979

**Kathryn R. Greenwold**
2240 Niskayuna Drive
Niskayuna, NY 12309
Phone: 1-518-370-1667

**Carolyn Maruggi**
51 Tobey Court
Pittsford, NY 14534
Phone: 1-716-385-1905

Carolyn Maruggi follows conservation guidelines in restoring quilts.

**Elizabeth Prokop**
Quilt Care
28 Broadway
Valhalla, NY 10595
Phone: 1-914-946-3358
1-914-946-7108

Elizabeth Prokop restores antique quilts, prepares quilts for hanging, replaces old bindings, ties tops and sells antique quilts.

*Pennsylvania*

**Helen Berger**
141 Cedarbrook Avenue
Ardmore, PA 19003
Phone: 1-215-649-4344

Helen Berger specializes in silk and Crazy Quilt restorations and uses both restoration and conservation methods.

**Sandra Cinfo**
Ye Olde Sewing Emporium
Rt. 191, St. John's Centre
P.O. Box 190
Hamlin, PA 18427
Phone: 1-717-689-3480

Sandra Cinfo has been restoring and finishing antique quilts for 20 years.

**M. Finkel and Daughter**
936  Pine Street
Philadelphia, PA 19107
Phone: 1-215-627-7797

The Finkels use museum-approved procedures to mount textiles onto acid free materials and offer restoration services for all antique textiles.

## Rhode Island

**Barbara Barber**
34 Langworthy Road
Westerly, RI 02891
Phone: 1-401-322-7906

## Vermont

**Pat Karambay**
Northfield Quilts
P.O. Box 7
Northfield, VT 05663
Phone: 1-802-485-6847

Pat Karamby has been doing quilt restoration for eight years.

## Virginia

**Barbara Smead**
102 First Patent Ct.
Williamsburg, VA 23188
Phone: 1-804-258-5779

The owner of Classics in Cotton quilt shop, Barbara Smead, has been restoring quilts for about ten years.

## Washington

**Marilyn Bacon**
10133 236th Place, SW
Edmonds, WA 98020
Phone: 1-206-546-8255

Marilyn Bacon is a third generation quilter and has been doing quilt restoration for 11 years.  Marilyn is very familiar with conservation techniques.

**Kathleen Butts**
N.E. 630 Illinois Street
Pullman, WA 99163
Phone: 1-509-332-2863

**Lorraine Torrence**
2112 South Spokane Street
Seattle, WA 98144
Phone: 1-206-725-8687

Lorraine Torrence teaches quilting and restores quilts privately and professionally for In The Beginning quilt shop.

## West Virginia

**Margaret Meadow**
Route 6, P.O.B. 109
Princeton, WV 24740
Phone: 1-304-425-6774

Margaret Meadow, restorer of quilts for seven years, uses conservation techniques when applicable.

# Bibliography

## Books

**Affleck, Diane L. Fagan,** *Just New From the Mills.* North Andover, MA: Museum of American Textile History, 1987.

*America's Quilts.* New York, NY: Gallery Books, W.H. Smith, 1990.

**Anderson, Suzy McLennan,** *Collector's Guide to Quilts.* Radnor, PA: Wallace Homestead, 1991.

*The Art of Dressmaking.* New York, NY: The Butterick Publishing Co., 1927.

**Beyer, Jinny,** *Patchwork Patterns.* McLean, VA: EPM Publications, Inc., 1979.

**Bishop, Robert,** *New Discoveries in American Quilts.* New York, NY: E.P. Dutton & Co., Inc., 1975.

**Bishop, Robert,** *Quilts, Coverlets, Rugs & Samplers.* New York, NY: Alfred A. Knopf, 1982.

**Bishop, Robert and Safanda, Elizabeth,** *A Gallery of Amish Quilts.* New York, NY: E. P. Dutton & Co., Inc., 1976.

**Brackman, Barbara,** *Clues in the Calico.* McLean, VA: EPM Publications, Inc., 1989.

**Carroll, Alice,** *The Good Housekeeping Needlecraft Encyclopedia.* New York, NY: Stamford House, 1947.

**Chase, Pattie and Dolbier, Mimi,** *The Contemporary Quilt.* New York, NY: E. P. Dutton & Co., Inc., 1978.

**Chatterton, Pauline,** *Patchwork and Applique.* New York, NY: The Dial Press, 1977.

**Cooper, Patricia and Buferd, Norma Bradley,** *The Quilters Women and Domestic Art.* Garden City, NY: Anchor Press/Doubleday, 1978.

**Duke, Dennis and Harding, Deborah,** *America's Glorious Quilts.* New York, NY: Park Lane, 1989.

**Earle, Alice Morse,** *Home Life in Colonial Days.* New York, NY: Macmillan Company, 1898.

**Fairservice, Jr., Walter,** *Costumes of the East.* Riverside, CT: The Chatham Press, Inc., 1971.

**Fangal, Esther; Winckler, Ida and Madsen, Agnete Wuldern,** *Danish Pulled Thread Embroidery.* New York, NY: Dover Publications, Inc., 1977.

**Fanning, Robbie and Tony,** *The Complete Book of Machine Quilting.* Radnor, PA: Chilton Book Co., 1980.

**Finch, Karen and Putnam, Greta,** *The Care and Preservation of Textiles.* Berkeley, CA: Lacis, 1991.

**Fons, Marianne and Porter, Liz,** *Quilter's Complete Guide.* Birmingham, AL: Oxmoor House, 1993.

**Foote, MD, Estelle,** *The Mender's Manual of Repairing and Preserving Garments and Bedding.* New York, NY: Harcourt Brace, Jovanovich, 1976.

**Fox, Sandi,** *Wrapped in Glory: Figurative Quilts & Bedcovers.* New York, NY: Thames and Hudson, 1990.

Greenbacker, Liz, and Barach, Kathleen, *Quilts —The First & Only Guide to Affordable 19th & 20th Century Quilts.* New York, NY: Avon Books, 1992.

Hall, Carrie A. and Kretsinger, Rose G., *The Romance of the Patchwork Quilt in America.* Caldwell, ID: The Caxton Printers, Ltd., 1947.

Herbort, Diane and Greenhut, Susan, *Old Glories: Magical Makeovers for Vintage Textiles, Trims and Photos.* McLean, VA: EPM Publications, Inc., 1992.

Holstein, Jonathan, *The Pieced Quilt–An American Design Tradition.* Greenwich, CT: New York Graphic Society Ltd., 1973.

Ickis, Marguerite, *The Standard Book of Quilt Making and Collecting.* New York, NY: Dover Publications, Inc., 1949.

Irwin, John Rice, *A People and Their Quilts.* Atglen, PA: Schiffer Publishing Co., 1984.

Isaacs, Jennifer, *200 Years of Australian Women's Domestic & Decorative Arts –The Gentle Arts.* New York, NY: Lansdowne Press, 1987.

Kafka, Francis, J., *The Hand Decoration of Fabric.* New York, NY: Dover Publications, Inc., 1959.

Kiracofe, Roderick, text with Mary Elizabeth Johnson, *The American Quilt: A History of Cloth and Comfort 1750-1950.* New York, NY: Clarkson Potter, 1993.

Kolter, Jane Bentley, *Forget Me Not –A Gallery of Friendship & Album Quilts.* Pittstown, NJ: The Main Street Press, 1985.

Lane, Rose Wilder, *Woman's Day Book of American Needlework.* New York, NY: Simon and Schuster, 1963.

Lewis, Alfred Allan, *The Mountain Artisans Quilting Book.* New York, NY: Macmillan Publishing Co., Inc., 1973.

Liddell, Jill and Watanabe, Yuko, *Japanese Quilts.* New York, NY: E. P. Dutton & Co., Inc., 1988.

Lipman, Jean and Winchester, Alice, *The Flowering of American Folk Art, (1776 - 1876).* New York, NY: Penguin Books, 1977.

Major, Connie, *Contemporary Patchwork Quilts: A stitch in our time.* New York, NY: Sterling Publishing Co., Inc., 1982.

Margolis, Adele P., *The Complete Book of Tailoring.* Garden City, NY: Doubleday & Co., Inc., 1978.

McKim, Ruth Short, *101 Patchwork Patterns.* New York, NY: Dover Publications, Inc., 1962.

McMorris, Penny and Kile, Michael, *The Art Quilt.* San Francisco, CA: The Quilt Digest Press, 1986.

McMorris, Penny, *Crazy Quilts.* New York, NY: E. P. Dutton & Co., Inc., 1984.

Meller, Susan and Eiffers, Joast, *Textile Designs.* New York, NY: Harry Abrams, Inc., 1991.

Newman, Thelma; Scott, Lee and Hartley, Jay, *Sewing Machine Embroidery and Stitchery.* New York, NY: Crown Publishers, Inc., 1980.

Noma, Seiroku, *The Heibonsha Survey of Japanese Art–Japanese Costume and Textile Arts.* New York, NY: Weathervane/Heibonsha, 1974.

Orlofsky, Patsy and Myron, *Quilts in America.* New York, NY: McGraw Hill, 1974.

**Peck, Amelia,** *American Quilts & Coverlets in The Metropolitan Museum of Art.* New York, NY: Dutton Studio Books, 1990.

**Pellman, Rachel and Kenneth,** *Amish Crib Quilts.* Intercourse, PA: Good Books, 1985.

**Pellman, Rachel T.,** *Amish Quilt Patterns.* Intercourse, PA: Good Books, 1984.

**Puentes, Nancy O'Brien,** *First Aid for Family Quilts.* Wheatridge, CO: Moon Over The Mountain Publishing Co., 1986.

*Quilt Digest Press.* San Francisco, CA: Quilt Digest Press, 1986.

**Rae, Janet,** *The Quilts of the British Isles.* London, England: Constable, 1987.

**Safford, Carleton, L. and Bishop, Robert,** *America's Quilts and Coverlets.* New York, NY: Weathervane Books, 1974.

**Segawa, Setsuko,** *Japanese Quilt Art.* Kyoto, Japan: Mitsumura Suiko Shoin, 1985.

**Seward, Linda,** *Successful Quilting.* Emmaus, PA: Rodale Press, 1987.

**Simms, Ami,** *Invisible Applique.* Flint, MI: Mallery Press, 1988.

**Simms, Ami,** *Classic Quilts Patchwork Designs From Ancient Rome.* Flint, MI: Mallery Press, 1991.

**Solvit, Marie-Janine,** *Les Appliques.* Paris, France: Dessain et Tolra, 1980.

**Solvit, Marie-Janine,** *Le Patchwork.* Paris, France: Dessain et Tolra, 1976.

**Thomas, Mary,** *Dictionary of Embroidery Stitches.* New York, NY: Gramercy Publishing Co., 1935.

**Wentworth, Judy,** *Quilts.* New York, NY: Crescent Books, 1989.

**Wooster, Ann Sargent,** *Quiltmaking–The Modern Approach to a Traditional Craft.* New York, NY: Drake Publishers, Inc., 1972.

**Woodard, Thomas K. and Greenstein, Blanche,** *Crib Quilts and Other Small Wonders.* New York, NY: E. P. Dutton & Co., Inc., 1981.

**Woodard, Thomas K. and Greenstein, Blanche,** *Twentieth Century Quilts 1900-1950.* New York, NY: E. P. Dutton & Co., Inc., 1988.

## Articles

"Altered States." *Antiques & Arts Weekly,* The Bee Publishing Company, (March 19, 1993): 56.

**Anonymous,** "How Much Piecin' A Quilt Is Like Living A Life." *Stitch 'N Sew Quilts,* no. 4 (May/June 1982): 21.

**Barnes, Genie,** "What's in the Sandwich?" *American Quilter,* (Winter 1988): 46.

**Beyer, Jinny,** "Preventing Color Fading in Fabrics." *The Keepsake Quilter,* vol. 4 (Spring 1991): 4-29.

**Bianco, Gina,** "Notes from the Conservator." *Quilt Connection,* vol. V, no. 2 (Spring 1993): 4.

**Brackman, Barbara,** "Old Tops: To Quilt or Not?" *Quilter's Newsletter Magazine,* (May 1986): 26-27.

Brackman, Barbara, "Seven Myths About Old Quilts." *Quilter's Newsletter Magazine*, vol. 19, no. 4 (April 1988): 40-57.

Brackman, Barbara, "Turkey Red in Quilts." *Quilter's Newsletter Magazine*, vol. 24, no. 2 (March 1992): 32-35.

Brackman, Barbara, "Who Was Aunt Martha?" *Quilter's Newsletter Magazine*, vol. 22, no. 5 (June 1991): 42-43.

Brackman, Barbara, "Who Was Nancy Page?" *Quilter's Newsletter Magazine*, vol. 22, no. 7 (September 1991): 22-23.

Brown, Becky, "A Shared Treasure." *American Quilter*, vol. IV, no. 2 (Summer 1988): 13.

Crowley, Carol, "Mending Stitches." *Quilter's Newsletter Magazine*, vol. 22, no. 4 (May 1991): 22.

David, Mrs. Thomas, "Using Up The Scraps." *The Household*, vol. 18, no. 3 (March 1918): 10.

Dedera, Sharon, "Keeper of the Canvas." *Antiques & Collecting*, vol. 98, no. 2 (April 1993): 36-39.

Eines, Donna Hanson, "New Life for 'Uglies'." *Quilting Today*, issue 27, (October/November 1991): 11.

Ferrero, Pat; Hedges, Elaine and Silber, Julie, "The Boon of the Sewing Machine." *Quilter's Newsletter Magazine*, (February 1990): 22.

Fox, Sandi, "Comments from the Quilt." *Modern Maturity*, vol. 33, no. 4 (August-September 1990): 58-63.

Goddu, Carol, "Relief Applique for Pictorial Quilts." *American Quilter*, vol. VI, no. 1 (Spring 1990): 48-50.

Gray, Paul, "An Ode to the Big Book." *Time*, (February 8, 1993): 66.

Greenbacker, Elizabeth, "Two Quilts from the Dump." *Stitch 'N Sew Quilts*, (January/February 1986): 16.

Haggerty-Jacobs, Ann, "Challenge-Olde is New." *American Quilter*, vol. V, no. 2 (Summer 1989): 30-33.

Harris, Betsy, "At Home With Quilts." *Quilter's Newsletter Magazine*, vol. 24, no. 3 (April 1992): 60-62.

Hearn, Linda, M., "Resurrecting a Family Treasure." *Quilting Today*, issue 29 (April 1992): 5-6.

Herdle, Becky, "Old Tops Equal New Quilts." *American Quilter*, vol. IV, no. 3 (Fall 1988): 14-17.

Hultgren, Sharon, "Truly A Victorian Treasure." *American Quilter*, vol. VI, no. 3 (Fall 1990): 22.

Jailer, Mildred, "The Successful Bible for The Happy Housewife." *Antiques and Collecting Hobbies*, vol. 97, no. 12 (February 1993): 18-20.

Kami, "Don't Judge a Quilt by its Condition." *The Hudson Valley Antiquer*, (November 1992): 13-14.

Kami, "K & K Quilteds: Not a Traditional Quilt Shop." *Quilting Today*, no. 11 (February/March 1989): 42-43.

**Kami,** "Quilt Restoration At Home." *Lady's Circle Quilt Craft,* vol. 2, no. 2 (June 1992): 34-36.

**Kami,** "Understanding Common Dye Problems." *The Hudson Valley Antiquer,* (February 1993): 3-7.

**Kerschner, Richard L.,** "Caring For The Extra Ordinary-Handling, Display and Cleaning of Antique Textiles." *Lady's Circle Patchwork Quilts,* (October 1993): 24-27.

**King, Helen,** "Roses Recycled." *Quilt World,* (March/April 1984): 24-25.

**Kitsen, Mary Louise,** "Quilts in History." *Quilt World,* (May/June 1981): 12-13.

**Lehman, Libby,** "Applique Over Patchwork." *American Quilter,* vol. VIII, no. 3 (Fall 1992): 22-25.

**LeMay, Chloe,** "Quilt Washday." *Quilter's Newsletter Magazine,* vol. 23, no. 10 (December 1991): 11.

**MacDonagh, Sandra,** "Patchwork & the Godey's Lady." *Quilt World,* (January-February 1982): 6-9.

**Madley, Carol Ann,** "A Letter From Martha Oliver Smith's Great Grandaughter." *Quilter's Newsletter Magazine,* vol. 19, no. 6 (June 1988): 14.

**Mangiapane, John,** "Victorian Crazy Quilting." *Quilt World Omni Book,* (Christmas Special 1982): 44.

**McElderry, Shirley,** "Repairing Older Quilts and Tops."*American Quilter,* vol. VIII, no 1, (Spring 1992): 38-40.

**Morris, Patricia,** "Stressing The Tradition: Julia Needham." *American Quilter,* vol.III, no. 4 (Winter 1987): 41.

**Oravecz, Cindy Zlotnik,** "Zen and the Art of Quilt Making." *Quilter's Newsletter Magazine,* vol. 24, no. 3 (April 1992): 16.

**Ostlere, Hilary,** "Silk is Still Queen." *Victoria,* (March 1993): 92-95.

**Porter, Liz,** "Broderie Perse Updated." *American Quilter,* vol. III, no. 1 (Spring 1991): 48-50.

**Rupp, Rebecca,** "Fashionable Calico." *Early American Life,* vol. XXIII, no. 3 (June 1992): 48-53.

**Rybicki, Verena,** "The Mill Girls of Lowell." *Traditional Quilter,* October 1990): 16-18.

**Simpson, Richard V.,** "Cuspidors a.k.a. Spittoons." *Antiques & Collecting,* vol. 97, no. 12 (February 1993): 22-23, 72.

**Spears, Jeannie M.,** "From Past to Present Renewing Old Quilt Tops." *Quilter's Newsletter Magazine,* vol. 25, no. 7 (September 1993): 52-53.

**Spears, Jeannie,** "Where In The World." *Lady's Circle Patchwork Quilts,* no. 85 (December 1992): 30-35.

**Stewart, Helma S.,** "Floral Applique: Making A Three Dimensional Rose." *American Quilter,* vol. III, no. 1 (Spring 1991): 18-21.

**Trager, Judith,** "Turkey Red Clues." *Quilter's Newsletter Magazine,* vol. 22, no. 8 (October 1991): 50-51.

**Trucco, Terry,** "Taking Care of Antique Quilts." *The New York Times,* (October 4, 1990): 47.

**Vaughn, Ciba,** "A Quilter's Odyssey." *Victoria,* (September 1992): 78-81.

**Wagner, Carol,** "Label and Document Your Quilt." *American Quilter,* vol. V, no. 1 (Spring 1989): 54-55.

**Wagner, Carol,** "Tips on Washing Quilts." *Quilting Today,* no. 10 (December/January 1989): 22.

**Ward, Kent,** "Old Before Their Time–Hints On Giving Your Quilts An Antique Look." *Quilting Today,* no. 25 (June/July 1991): 8-9.

**Watkins, Ann M.,** "If Quilts Could Talk." *Quilting Today,* no. 14 (August/September 1989): 11.

**Waz, Deidre,** "North Andover Conservators Preserve Treasures of the Diamond." *Massachusetts Bay Antiques,* (July 1993): 21-28.

**Wilhide, Elizabeth,** "William Morris–A Quilt to Realize The Beauty of Life." *Victoria,* (September 1992): 91-95.

**Wittles, Anne,** "The Quilt: Versatile and Enduring." *Quilt World,* (Christmas Annual, 1973): 14.

**Wolf, Lois,** "Natural Fabric Dyeing, The Forgotten Art." *Quilting Today,* no. 13 (June/July 1989): 22-23.

**Young, Susan,** "Sister Quilts from Sicily–A Pair of Renaissance Bedcovers." *Quilter's Newsletter Magazine,* vol. 25, no. 7 (September 1993): 41-43.

**Yorko, Aloyse,** "The Garbage Can Quilt and Other Lonelies." *Quilter's Newsletter Magazine,* vol. 21, no. 2 (February 1990): 26-28.

**Zegart, Shelly,** "Buying Old Quilts." *American Quilter,* (Fall 1990): 26.

# Reference Notes

1  Foote, p. 179

2  Irwin, pp. 26-7

3  Finch and Putnam, p. 91

4  Phone interview with Kaethe Kliot 8/11/93

5  Holstein, p. 83, p. 127

6  Hall & Kretsinger, p. 267

7  Brackman, p. 15, p. 16

8  Hearn, pp. 5-6

9  Yorko, pp. 26-8

10  Young, pp. 41-3

11  Spear, *Lady's Circle Patchwork Quilts*, p. 30

12  Ostlere, p. 92

13  Wilhide, pp. 91-5

14  Anderson, p. 112

15  Interview with quilt restorer, Susan Wilson  8/21/93

16  Zegart, p. 26

17  Herbort & Greenhut, p. 79, p. 83

18  Finch & Putnam, p. 91

19  Anderson, p. 87

20  Meller & Eiffers, the entire book

21  McElderry, pp. 38-40

22  Holstein, p. 46 caption

23  McElderry, p. 40

24  Goddu, p. 49

25  Stewart, p. 19

26  Gray, p. 66

27  Simpson, p. 22

28  "Altered States", p. 56

29  Spears,  Quilter's Newsletter Magazine, p. 52

30  Greenbacker & Barach, p. 92

31  Holstein, pp. 7-8

32  Holstein, p. 84

33  Brackman, p. 129

34  Spears, *Quilter's Newsletter Magazine*, p. 54

35  Wentworth, p. 7

36  Finch & Putnam, p. 17

37  Larcom, p. 191

38  Carroll, p. 42

39  McElderry, p. 40. Simms, *Invisible Applique* also refers to the ladder stitch which McElderry favors; yet Simms herself thanks Lola Choinski for showing her the ladder stitch.

40  Carroll, p. 431

41  Carroll, p. 437

42  Carroll, p. 104

43  Irwin, p. 140

44  Irwin, p. 143

45  Puentes, pp. 20-2

46  Beyer, *The Keepsake Quilter*, pp. 4-29

47  Greenbacker & Barach, p. 118

48  Wagner, p. 22

49  LeMay, p. 11

50  Greenbacker & Barach, p. 112

51  *The Art of Dressmaking*, p. 246

52  *The Art of Dressmaking*, p. 245

53  *The Art of Dressmaking*, p. 245

54  McMorris, p. 115, Puentes, p. 19

55  Bishop, *Quilts, Coverlets, Rugs, & Samplers*, p. 41

56  Finch & Putnam, pp. 84-90

# *Many Thanks*

THIS BOOK would not have been possible without the help of many quilt enthusiasts who shared their collections and expertise over the last ten years. My deepest thanks to Jane Lury for her Labors of Love collection, Jack and Michelle Cassella, George and Connie Colclough, Country Curtains collection, Mike Fallon, Laura Fisher, Joseph Flummerfelt, Josephine Gage, Robert and Ardis James, Andrea Krapit, Claudia Kingsley, Olive and Sonya Langdon, Helen Lampman, John Sauls, Maureen Sheehan, Ingrid Wheeler, Shelly Zegart via Joseph and Joan Boyle, Larry Zingale, Columbia County Quilt Guild.

Robert and Estelle Stetson for their vast textile information.

Karl W. Blodgett for his months of computer time and expertise in helping to prepare this manuscript. Lisa de Conti and Gabrielle Cognac for hours of tedious typing and collating information. Daniel K. Blodgett and Sylvia Ayers for their patient handling of details. David Blodgett for co-ordinating photo sessions with Henry Edgeworth and Blair Benken.

Marion Martin whose diligent search for perfect vintage fabrics and antique quilting information is ongoing.

The constant parade of American quilts displayed at Copake Country Auction, Copake, NY; Caropreso Gallery, Great Barrington, MA; Bradford Auction, Sheffield, MA; Tom Gage Auction, S. Egremont, MA. A special thanks to these auction houses for their help as a never-ending source of vintage fabrics and quilt memorabilia.

The many quilt owners around the country who entrusted their damaged quilts to the quilt restoration studio, K & K Quilteds in Hillsdale, NY.

## *About the Author*

CAMILLE DALPHOND COGNAC grew up on the textile history of Lowell, Massachusetts. Surrounded by fabric from the time of her birth, Camille (known as Kami) absorbed the skills of fine upholstery and dressmaking from her father and mother while she pursued a classical education. She earned an MA in English literature, then taught and researched here and in Europe before returning to textiles.

Starting in 1974 and while rearing three sons, she worked as a free lance writer and fiber artist specializing in one-of-a-kind clothing and wall art. Her commissioned wall quilts hang in private collections throughout the world. They, along with the prizes she was winning, brought her so many requests for help in repairing heirloom quilts that she and her friend Kittie Becker, opened a studio known as K & K Quilteds in Hillsdale, New York in 1982.

Soon damaged quilts were arriving at the rate of one a day, and their library of vintage fabrics had become so vast that K & K became the nation's largest on-site restoration studio. Featured in quilt and antiques magazines, K & K also went on television. Their show was chosen best of series for 1993 by Albany's Channel 10. Through her personal networking with many restorers, quilt historians, manufacturers of fabrics and other necessary supplies, Kami saw the need for bringing the entire restoration family together. Before she had finished writing QUILT RESTORATION, she had founded the Quilt Restoration Society and begun editing the QRS Newsletter.

Sharing age-old restoration techniques and describing the latest contemporary ways to reformat quilts give her joy that pulses throughout her writing. Its intensity is matched only by the pleasure she takes in helping to renew the life of a beloved damaged quilt.